WHAT Every **5**th **Grade Teacher** Needs to Know

About Setting Up AND Running a Classroom

Mike Anderson

NORTHEAST FOUNDATION FOR CHILDREN, INC.

All net proceeds from the sale of this book support the work of Northeast Foundation for Children, Inc. (NEFC). NEFC, a not-for-profit educational organization, is the developer of the *Responsive Classroom*® approach to teaching, which fosters safe, challenging, and joyful elementary classrooms and schools.

The stories in this book are all based on real events in the classroom. However, to respect the privacy of students, their names and many identifying characteristics have been changed.

ISBN: 978-1-892989-45-1

Library of Congress Control Number: 2010927986

Cover and book design by Helen Merena.
Photographs by Jeff Woodward and Peter Wrenn. All rights reserved.

Thanks to the teachers and students of Garfield Elementary School, Springfield, Virginia; Kensington Avenue Elementary School, Springfield, Massachusetts; Six to Six Magnet School, Bridgeport, Connecticut; and Stafford Elementary School, Stafford Springs, Connecticut, who welcomed Northeast Foundation for Children to take photos in their classrooms.

Northeast Foundation for Children, Inc.
85 Avenue A, Suite 204
P.O. Box 718
Turners Falls, MA 01376-0718

800-360-6332
www.responsiveclassroom.org

15 14 13 12 11   7 6 5 4 3 2 1

CONTENTS

Knowing Fifth Graders

I had taught fourth grade for four years and decided that I could keep on teaching it for the rest of my career. I had no interest in changing grades. Then, in the spring, our principal announced that our school needed another fifth grade teacher for next year to bring class sizes down a bit. She wanted to know if any teacher in the school wanted to take the new fifth grade spot.

The current group of fourth graders I taught was a tough one—the most challenging class I'd had in my short career. But they had just gelled as a class and were turning into an incredibly strong learning community. I went to the principal and asked if I could move up with this group of fourth graders. She agreed, and I was thrilled. My journey as a fifth grade teacher had begun.

That class still stands out in my mind. They had great energy and unique personalities. They were funny and goofy and earnest and a handful all at the same time. I learned so many new things as a teacher as I moved with this class from fourth to fifth grade.

Know Where Students Are Developmentally

First of all, I learned that fifth graders aren't just slightly bigger fourth graders. Besides showing physical changes, these children also tend to be different from their fourth grade selves in the social-emotional, cognitive, and language realms. That this is so shouldn't come as a surprise for teachers. Research tells us, and the experiences of seasoned teachers confirm, that children grow and develop on multiple fronts at once. Just as children's physical characteristics (height, weight, physical coordination, eyesight, and so on) change, so, too,

1

do other characteristics, such as attention span, friendship preferences, ability to think abstractly, and sense of humor. When we understand the common characteristics of fifth graders, we can create classroom spaces, design lessons, and group children in ways that are especially appropriate for them.

Common Characteristics of Fifth Graders

I sometimes joke that as an extrovert, I often need to talk to think. Many fifth graders seem to share that need. Whether working on math problems, walking in the hallways, conducting a science experiment, riding on the school bus, or waiting for an assembly to begin, fifth graders generally love to chat. Of course, we could say this of just about any age (and for adults as well as children), but in fifth grade, this characteristic seems especially prominent.

This need to talk constantly can be a real challenge if one of our goals is to have a quiet classroom and school environment. And while the importance of a quiet school environment is often overemphasized, I think that most educators would agree that a generally calm and quiet classroom helps children to concentrate and feel safe. So what might school look like if we leveraged the super-chattiness of fifth graders in ways that could help with their learning?

Here's what I do: I group students together at desks and tables in small collaborative clusters, spaced apart from one another. I use interactive modeling (discussed in detail in Chapter 2) to teach fifth graders how to use quiet voices while talking in the hallways and then let them walk in pairs instead of in single file. And I incorporate partner-chats, peer conferences, and other collaborative structures into daily lessons in all subjects. Rather than spend time and energy trying to keep fifth graders quiet, I teach them how and when to talk productively. If you think of fifth graders' common charac-

Rather than spend time and energy trying to keep fifth graders quiet, I teach them how and when to talk productively. If you think of fifth graders' common characteristics as assets, not liabilities, you can use them to help students capitalize on their strengths.

teristics as assets, not liabilities, you can use them to help students capitalize on their strengths.

The inclination to talk is just one characteristic that many fifth graders share. In general, they also can take on more complex work in school, are becoming more focused on peer relationships, and can think more abstractly.

The table on pages 4–6 highlights some of the most common characteristics of fifth graders. As you explore this table, it's important to keep these ideas in mind:

■ **Human development is complex.** Even scientists who study it do not fully agree on the means by which humans grow socially, emotionally, linguistically, or cognitively. Most theorists describe the process as a dynamic interaction between a person's biological disposition and many environmental factors—including the historical era in which a person grows up, the person's culture and family, and the institutions he or she encounters (such as schools, places of worship, and the media). The table is not intended to ignore this complexity. Instead, it offers you a bridge between the abstract ideas of theory and their practical expression in children's classroom behavior.

■ **Every child is unique.** As a result of the complex and dynamic process of development, no two children—not even identical twins with the same genetic makeup—will develop in the same way or at the same rate. And for many children, one area may develop at a much faster rate than another. For example, a particular fifth grader might have social-emotional behaviors that are very common among fourth graders (such as preferring to play or work with one or two friends and being less concerned with "popular" trends or social status). But that child may also have cognitive behaviors more like those of a sixth grader (such as more advanced math or reading skills). Finally, it's important to keep in mind that the traits listed in the table should never limit your thinking about a student's potential. There will always be individuals with capabilities beyond those considered typical; not every child will fit neatly into the categories outlined here.

3

■ **The table gives you a practical frame of reference.** It lets you prepare for teaching fifth graders and gives you a resource if something puzzling comes up. For instance, once you start teaching fifth grade, you may notice that some students keep complaining about being hungry in the middle of the morning, even though they ate breakfast and have the earliest lunch. Once you know that many fifth graders are experiencing growth spurts and struggling to maintain their energy levels, you might adjust to this developmental need by introducing a snack option that allows them to eat while they work (within certain guidelines you set). Instead of getting frustrated with this or any other behavior, use your knowledge of fifth graders' common characteristics to develop practical solutions that support their healthy growth and development.

To learn more about child development, see the resources in the "About Child Development" section, starting on page 121.

Fifth Graders

Common Characteristics	School Implications
Social-Emotional	
■ Generally happy; enjoy family, peers, and teachers.	■ Build group work into lessons, activities, and projects. (Flexible groups can work well; students can work with lots of different people, including adults and peers.)
■ Work well in groups.	
■ Usually truthful; developing a more mature sense of right and wrong.	■ Expect arguments (and that they will tend to end quickly).
■ Sensitive to and able to resolve issues of fairness.	■ Encourage their developing sense of fairness and of right and wrong. (These can lead to lively class debates and discussions.)
■ Able to enjoy cooperative and competitive games.	■ Provide opportunities for peer tutoring, book buddies, and development of conflict resolution and other interpersonal skills.

Fifth Graders

Common Characteristics	School Implications
Physical	
■ Large muscles developing quickly. ■ Drawn to the outdoors and physical challenges. ■ Handwriting may become messier than in fourth grade. ■ Due to growth spurts, frequently hungry and can tire easily.	■ Set up schedules to include sufficient time for recess (and other outdoor play), energizers and other movement breaks, snacks, and lunch. ■ Consider a snack option that enables students to eat and work in the classroom. ■ Provide instruction and practice for use of tools such as rulers, compasses, and computers.
Cognitive	
■ Good at memorizing facts. ■ Increasingly able to think abstractly; good at solving problems. ■ Enjoy rules and logic. ■ Enjoy collecting, classifying, and organizing. ■ Take pride in schoolwork. ■ Able to concentrate for longer periods of time.	■ Structure complex projects with proper scaffolding and guidance to build on their abilities to be highly productive with schoolwork. ■ Give ongoing encouragement and reinforcement for both effort and results. ■ Include lessons that help build their memory skills (for example, practicing math facts and learning facts about geography, history, and world records). ■ Support classification and other organizational skills with hands-on science work and math projects.

5

CONTINUED ▷

Common Characteristics	School Implications
Language	
■ Expressive and talkative.	■ Encourage students to verbalize their thinking to help make discussions, debates, book groups, writing conferences, math groups, and so on more productive.
■ Like to explain things.	
■ Able to listen well.	
■ Interest in reading independently becomes stronger.	■ Provide opportunities for choral reading, singing, reciting poetry, and performing skits and plays.
	■ Include time for independent reading and writing.

The information in this chart is based on *Yardsticks: Children in the Classroom Ages 4–14,* 3rd ed., by Chip Wood (Northeast Foundation for Children, 2007), and is consistent with the following sources:

Child Development Guide by the Center for Development of Human Services, SUNY, Buffalo State College. 2002.
WWW.BSC-CDHS.ORG/FOSTERPARENTTRAINING/PDFS/CHILDDEVELGUIDE.PDF

"The Child in the Elementary School" by Frederick C. Howe, *Child Study Journal,* Vol. 23, Issue 4. 1993.

Your Child: Emotional, Behavioral, and Cognitive Development from Birth through Preadolescence by AACAP (American Academy of Child and Adolescent Psychiatry) and David Pruitt, MD. Harper Paperbacks. 2000.

What about Developmentally Younger and Older Fifth Graders?

Of course, in any classroom, you'll have students of various ages and at various points along the developmental path. The tallest student in the class may seem younger socially. A student who is younger chronologically may be a stronger reader. Some fifth graders may display characteristics more often displayed by students in fourth grade or sixth grade. Or they may display characteristics of multiple grades, depending on their growth and development in a particular area. You may even have enough students at a similar point in their development to make the class as a whole feel "younger" or "older."

Certainly, you'll see a shift as the year progresses. Springtime fifth graders will be a different bunch than they were at the start of school. Again, all children are different and each class is different. Still, there can be some characteristics that you would expect to see in fifth graders who are developmentally younger (more like fourth graders) or those who are developmentally older (more like sixth graders).

Younger fifth graders may:

■ **Prefer smaller work and play groups.** When younger fifth graders can work in partnerships, rather than groups of four or five, they may have more positive social interactions and do more productive academic work.

■ **Be a bit more tense and anxious.** It's helpful for younger fifth grade students if you're extra careful to explain directions step by step, stick to your schedule, and break larger projects into bite-sized tasks.

■ **Have a shorter attention span.** Younger fifth graders will benefit from shorter lessons and work periods and from frequent movement breaks. They may also tire more quickly, so several short breaks throughout the day are better than one long one in the middle of the day.

■ **Still be very concrete learners.** Younger fifth graders may not understand subtle humor. They will likely need to use math manipulatives or pictures to work through more abstract concepts (such as long division or different historical perspectives).

Older fifth graders may:

■ **Push back on adult authority.** Older fifth graders may be more combative and argumentative. They need adults to remain empathetic and keep their sense of humor.

■ **Be growing.** A lot. Students in the throes of growth spurts need frequent rests, snack breaks, and physical activity. Having healthy snacks on hand and scheduling short breaks can help them better focus on academic tasks.

■ **Be concerned with social dynamics.** This is the age for some students, especially girls, when who's in and who's out, who likes whom, and who is friends with whom become much more important.

■ **Begin to take broader perspectives.** As their thinking becomes increasingly complex, older fifth grade students are better able to see issues from multiple sides. They enjoy debates and arguing for their cause.

How to Use This Book

You might choose to use this book in a couple of ways. For example, you may want to:

■ **Read it cover to cover.** If you have time, and the start of the school year is still weeks away, you may want to read this book from start to finish. This approach can help you develop a "big picture" view of fifth grade while picking up many practical tips.

■ **Focus on something specific.** Perhaps you've been recently hired or transferred and will be teaching fifth grade in just a few days. If so, you might want to begin reading about how to set up the classroom and arrange the furniture in Chapter 1. On the other hand, you might be several weeks or months into the school year. In that case, you might start with the chapter that seems most relevant to your situation right now. For example, if the classroom community is struggling to come together, turn to Chapter 3. Or if you feel that students are ready for a big project or field trip, start with Chapter 4. Wherever you begin, you can always check out the other parts of the book when you have more time.

Regardless of how you use this book, consider implementing new ideas slowly. Making too many changes or setting too many goals all at once is likely to overwhelm you and the students. Try one or two new things at a time and get comfortable with them before moving on. Don't worry about making mistakes. The best teachers are also the best learners—ones who try new ideas, make some mistakes, learn from them, and try new ideas again.

Ready? Get Set . . .

Fifth grade is a year of such incredible growth and change! At the beginning of each school year, I'm always surprised at how small and young incoming fifth graders seem. And by the end of the year, I'm thrilled that so many fifth graders have grown and reached amazing new developmental milestones. It's incredible to observe these changes—noticing, for example, how some students struggle to see others' points of view in September and then seeing them carefully consider everyone's opinions during project work a few months later. Actively supporting this growth and development is one of the great joys of teaching fifth grade.

As the year moves along, you'll undoubtedly find yourself getting caught up in the many demands of the teaching profession. After all, there are standards to cover, phone calls to make, paperwork to fill out, and other tasks to complete. So, as you embark on the journey of teaching fifth graders, don't forget to really get to know and enjoy the students and their families. They're what make all the hard work so worthwhile!

. . . Go!

CHAPTER 1

Classroom Setup

Three different times in my career as a classroom teacher, I have had the opportunity to "loop"—to move from one school year to the next with the same group of students. At the end of one year with a group of fourth graders, we were having a class discussion about moving up to fifth grade together—a prospect that we were all excited about. As we were discussing various aspects of the transition, including what the room would physically look like, Yeji raised her hand, looking a bit puzzled. "Mr. Anderson, we're all going to be coming back to the same classroom with the same group of kids. Won't it kind of feel like fourth grade all over again?"

Yeji's question pointed to an important principle of setting up effective classrooms. To learn at their best, students need their physical classroom to fit their developmental characteristics and their learning activities. That means the room needs to look and feel different from year to year. Sure, some things may be similar in multiple grades—the structures of reading and writing workshops, for example—but there are also important differences between grades that need to be reflected in the ways we set up the classroom.

As you design a fifth grade classroom, ask yourself some questions: What kinds of work will the students be doing? How often will they be working together? What units are first, and what materials and workspaces will students need for this work? How big are the students and what are their needs for physical space? Where will students keep all of their supplies and personal things? These and many other similar questions should drive the particulars of how you arrange the room.

This chapter provides guidelines for setting up an effective learning environment for fifth grade students—how to arrange furniture, set up whole-class meeting spaces, provide appropriate classroom supplies, and create effective classroom displays. Besides meeting the unique needs of fifth graders, these ideas will help you create a learning environment that is interactive and child-centered—important considerations for any grade.

Arranging the Furniture

In fifth grade classrooms, I often see one of two seating arrangements. The first has students sitting at clusters of four desks, with all of the clusters positioned so that students can see the interactive whiteboard, dry erase board, or overhead projector screen. The other typical setup has students arranged in some variation of a horseshoe shape, again so that all students can see the screen or board that the teacher will be using. Each of these two setups is better than the traditional arrangement of student desks set in rows facing the chalkboard. However, each of these arrangements has drawbacks that can be challenging for fifth graders because each works against some key common characteristics of most students in this grade:

■ **Fifth graders tend to be very social.** Of course, we could say this of just about any grade. Yet around fifth grade, a key shift often happens with students' social interests: They often become much more concerned with peer relationships and friendships than they have been previously. This peer emphasis can work to their advantage academically: Learning tasks that involve debate, discussion, and collaboration  can be particularly fruitful in fifth grade. However, when we put all of the students in a fifth grade class together and facing in the same direction, it can be hard for them to disengage from social conversations when it's time to work. Small-group seating arrangements can be more effective, allowing students to work with others, but limiting the number of people in the immediate vicinity.

■ **To learn, fifth graders need to do.** Although fifth graders start to tackle more complex and higher-level academic tasks, they still learn more effectively through hands-on projects and active explorations than through lectures. Any classroom arrangement that has all the students' seats arranged facing the teacher at the board runs the risk of turning into a teacher-lecture-centered classroom.

So what's the ideal room set-up for fifth graders? I've found that scattering tables or small clusters of desks throughout the room and setting up a separate whole-class meeting space works best. This design allows students  to gather for direct instruction when necessary, while enabling them to spend most of their time engaged in independent and small-group work.

Whole-Group Meeting Area

When planning a classroom, the first thing I work on is a whole-group circle area. This circle is perfect for the three-part lesson structure that allows for dynamic and interactive learning in fifth grade. First, students gather in the circle for a short, whole-class lesson (about ten minutes). Second, students move to desks and tables to work on the skills taught during the lesson. Third, students return to the circle to reflect on their work. This type of structure also helps support fifth graders' need for movement.

I also find that the circle is a perfect place to gather with students and start off each day with a *Responsive Classroom*® Morning Meeting. In addition, the circle can serve as a place to meet for class discussions, to solve class problems, and to join together for the daily read-aloud. Plus, a circle area is also a great place to do an energizer, or short movement break (see page 69 to learn more about energizers).

Learn More about Morning Meeting at www.responsiveclassroom.org

The Morning Meeting Book by Roxann Kriete (Northeast Foundation for Children, 2002).

"Morning Meeting: A Powerful Way to Begin the Day," *Responsive Classroom Newsletter*, February 1999.

Here are some points to keep in mind when building a whole-group meeting area:

■ **Make sure it's big enough.** Some fifth graders are starting to take up as much space as some adults, so as you construct the circle, keep in mind that students need to be comfortable and not squished against each other.

13

■ **Plan where you'll write.** Some teachers use an easel placed in the perimeter of the circle. Others use an interactive whiteboard or an overhead projector. If you plan on using a circle area for instruction, make sure to include your teaching tool in your circle design. Sometimes, a projector works best when placed to the side of the circle where it can be moved in or out as needed (so a bulky cart isn't in the way while holding meetings or discussions).

■ **Plan where students sit.** I myself am more comfortable in a chair than I am on the floor, and I like to be on the same eye level as students, so I try to get chairs into the circle whenever possible. Chairs also help define each individual's personal space, which can help improve students' focus. I know other teachers who prefer teaching from the floor. Fifth graders can get uncomfortable quickly on the floor, though, especially if the floor is tiled, so think about keeping lessons short and active if students are on the floor.

■ **Assign seats early in the year.** Because fifth graders care deeply about friendships and social connections, assigning seats early in the year can help relieve some of the pressure to find the "right" seat in the circle. (I change the seating assignments frequently to help students get to know each other and build the classroom community.) Once the classroom community is feeling positive and safe, you can loosen up on this a bit, always keeping an eye on where students are sitting to make sure that cliques and exclusion aren't creeping in.

Desk and Table Seating

Once you've got the circle area planned out, it's time to figure out a seating arrangement. Whether you have desks, tables, or a combination, here are some ideas to keep in mind:

■ **Spread furniture apart.** Many fifth graders hit a major growth spurt at some point in the year. As students' bodies are stretching out, they tend to be a bit awkward and clumsy. (I've seen fifth grade boys standing perfectly still suddenly topple to the floor. It's as if one leg just grew a quarter of an inch and threw off their sense of balance!) If desks and tables are jammed together, students will bump into each other as they move about the room, knocking over projects, shaking desks, and causing general mayhem. Tempers will invariably flare. Also, as mentioned before, the more students are crammed into a single space, the more likely they are to get caught up in side conversations that may distract them from their work.

■ **Keep things flexible.** Few teachers ever complain of having too much space in their classrooms. Most of us wish our rooms were bigger, but this is rarely an option, so instead, we need to create classroom arrangements that are flexible. Make sure the computer area can be easily turned into a regular work space. Ensure that the circle area can also be used during work times. Once you teach your fifth graders how to move furniture safely and efficiently, you can shift desks and tables as needed throughout the day, since various subjects may require different configurations. For example, during a science lesson when students are using tubs of water to study

When Spreading Out Doesn't Work

If you're not able to create a circle area for direct teaching, students will need to sit where they can comfortably see you and any visuals you use. In that case, put the tables or small clusters of desks in the middle of the room. Be sure to give students movement breaks.

For an occasional change of scenery once you've finished your direct teaching, let students spread out to work on the floor, at other desks or tables, or in any workable space they feel comfortable using.

15

CONTINUED ON PAGE 18 ▶

"I Don't Have Room for a Circle!"

Unfortunately, the lack of classroom space is not an unusual challenge for teachers. If space is tight, try to at least gather the whole class in a circle once or twice a day for brief, community-building meetings. Here are some possible ways to do this:

1 Create a temporary meeting area.

At meeting time, the children move desks and other furniture to open up a large space for a circle. After the meeting, the students return the furniture to its original place. With adequate teaching and practice, children will be able to do this setup and takedown in just a few minutes.

Three keys to making a temporary meeting space work:

■ **Choose carefully.** Choose a spot with as little furniture as possible. Any furniture should be easy for students to move.

■ **Use props to define the area.** An easel pad, interactive whiteboard, or overhead projector can all work well. Ideally, these tools would stay put and serve as the point from which the meeting circle grows.

■ **Teach furniture moving.** Use interactive modeling to teach and practice how to move the furniture carefully, cooperatively, and quickly. Try turning the practice into a game, such as beating the clock.

2 Create it once, use it twice.

Have children move furniture to make room at the end of the day for a "closing circle," in which they reflect on their day, share about their work, or plan together for the following day. After the meeting, leave the space open—don't move any furniture back. The next morning, the space will be ready for a meeting that welcomes the children, affirms the strength of the classroom community, and warms them up for the day ahead. Once the morning meeting is completed, students move the furniture back. At the end of the day, they repeat this process.

3 Use a space outside the classroom.

Go to the cafeteria, library, gym, or other space in the school that's large enough to accommodate a circle. This solution, admittedly the most difficult, works best when you:

■ **Use the same space every day.** The familiarity will help children succeed.

■ **Limit distractions.** For example, if you use the cafeteria, meet when no other class is there.

■ **Meet at the same time every day.** Even if it's not the most ideal time, the predictability will help students focus and feel secure.

■ **Teach the expected behaviors.** Be sure to teach transition routines and behavioral expectations outside the classroom.

Interactive Modeling

See Chapter 2, "Schedules and Routines," for a full explanation of interactive modeling.

The whole-group meeting circle is the heart of classroom life. Sitting in a circle, everyone can see and be seen by everyone else. And because the circle has no beginning and no end, it allows everyone an equal place in the group. By the very nature of its design, the meeting circle invites group participation and fosters inclusion. Its presence and prominence in the classroom or in the school day, even if only temporary, says, "In this class, we value working together, and we value each individual's contributions to the group."

mass and volume, it might be best to have three big group areas where tables are pulled together. During the next period, students may be working on poetry, so you may want to have them spread out into smaller groups or use their own seats.

■ **Assign seats at the beginning of the year.** My preference is to help students get to the point where no seats are assigned. Instead, all space is shared and students sit at different spots throughout the day. It lends a nice democratic atmosphere to the room. However, I usually start the year with assigned seats. When nerves are high at the beginning of the year, not having to figure out where and with whom to sit can reduce anxiety for students. If you don't assign seats at the beginning of the year, at least direct students where to go as they move from lessons to work spots. ("Jimmy, Maya, Rico, and Jeannie, you four move to this table. Destaynee, John, Leslie, and Marlon, sit at the next table over.")

■ **Name table or desk groups.** It's nice to give specific names to seating groups so we have an easy way to address each group. Consider also how these names can reinforce content or values that we want to emphasize. While studying rocks and minerals, for instance, you might name table groups after vocabulary words: igneous, sedimentary, metamorphic, geology, and glaciers. When studying westward expansion, tables might be named Mississippi, Rockies, Great Plains, and so on. One school that I visited named classrooms after local colleges to help students see college as a goal, and this same idea could be used to name work tables.

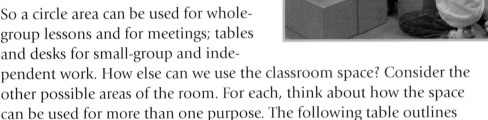

Other Areas of the Classroom

So a circle area can be used for whole-group lessons and for meetings; tables and desks for small-group and independent work. How else can we use the classroom space? Consider the other possible areas of the room. For each, think about how the space can be used for more than one purpose. The following table outlines some ideas.

Designing Multipurpose Spaces

Area	Tips	Multiple Uses
Classroom library	■ Arrange bookshelves with enough space so that many students can browse at once. ■ Try a horseshoe shape so the bookshelves create a cozy space big enough for a work table. ■ Place books in bins organized by author or subject so they're easy to browse.	■ Displaying books and storing literacy supplies ■ Doing guided reading or other small-group work ■ Holding one-on-one or small-group conferences ■ Doing regular classroom work ■ Doing small-group projects
Theme or content area	■ Have an area for books, displays, and ongoing work for science and social studies units. ■ Have a bulletin board or wall display space for rotating charts, posters, and photos of students.	■ Displaying theme work ■ Working on theme projects or assignments ■ Doing other classroom work
Computer area	■ Keep equipment safely stored when not in use. ■ Arrange desktop computers so keyboards can be easily moved.	■ Doing research or other computer work ■ Doing regular work when computers aren't in use
Storage area	■ Have shelves and cupboards for student supplies and materials. ■ Keep teacher-only supplies out of sight and out of reach. ■ Periodically clean out damaged and worn supplies.	■ Storing supplies ■ Hanging coats (place coat hooks on the backs of supply cabinets) ■ Displaying student work (on cabinet doors)

Add Some Homey Touches

Adding a few simple homey touches to a classroom can really warm it up and make it feel more safe and inviting for students. A few large plants can reduce noise, create a nice feel in the room, and help purify the air. A floor lamp or desk lamp can allow you to turn off some of the overhead fluorescents, which tend to shed a harsh light. A bird-feeder outside the window gives students a chance to observe nature and can make the classroom feel like it extends beyond the walls of the room. An area rug can cover worn tiles or spots in an old carpet while also defining an area of the classroom. Check online or in your local newspaper for used items that people are looking to give away, and follow school guidelines for adding any furnishings or other objects to the classroom.

Classroom Supplies

Fifth graders are capable of incredible work—it's one of the great joys of teaching this grade. I've seen fifth graders design professional looking presentations, write breathtakingly beautiful poetry, create complex three-dimensional historical maps, and produce and perform in engaging skits and short movies. Quality classroom supplies play a huge role in helping fifth graders do good work.

Here are some important issues to think about as you assemble supplies for your classroom:

Quality

Imagine the frustration of a fifth grader who is supposed to create high-quality maps, graphs, and other projects with markers that are dry, scissors that are too small, or reference books that are out-

---

No Budget for Supplies?

If your school does not give you a supply budget but instead relies on parents to provide supplies, you could replace the traditional shopping list with assignments so that each parent donates one category to the class. For example, one parent supplies the pencils, another some markers, and so forth.

Also, you could explore using a website set up to link interested donors with classrooms:

- WWW.DONORSCHOOSE.ORG
- WWW.ILOVESCHOOLS.COM
- WWW.ADOPTACLASSROOM.ORG

dated. To avoid that frustration and enable students to do good work, let's make sure that classroom supplies are of adequate quality. For example, markers should be bold and fresh. Scissors should be adult-sized and sharp. Clay should be moist and malleable. Books should have covers and clean pages and include old favorites as well as those by new authors or on current themes. Pencil sharpeners should actually sharpen pencils. High-quality supplies transmit to students an air of profession-

alism about the classroom and their work. They also tell students that we care about quality; we care about their work; we care about them.

Quantity

If we're going to have students working on projects that require them to cut, tape, glue, mold, and create, then we need to make sure there are enough necessary supplies to go around. If we don't, it shouldn't be surprising when arguments erupt as students vie for use of the limited supplies. If budgets are tight, consider sending out a request to parents and other community members to donate supplies.

Relevancy

Some supplies, such as markers, calculators, rulers, and paper, will be used throughout the year. Others, such as geoboards, microscopes, balance scales, and relief maps, may be more content-specific and thus not needed every day. It's best to put out only the supplies that are relevant to the curriculum you're studying. If students don't need access to microscopes, tuck these away, out of sight, until they're needed. You'll reduce clutter and ensure that students know what can and can't be used. If it's visible, it's fair game—if it's not visible, it's off-limits for now.

Shared by All

Although it might seem simple and logical to ask each student's family to provide the supplies the child will need, this can actually lead to problems in the classroom. Feelings of inequality and jealousy inevitably result when some students whose families can afford more expensive supplies bring those supplies into school. Worse yet, in fifth grade, when friendships and social dynamics can take on new urgency for students, some students may share supplies with their three or four best friends, but not with others.

Instead of this divisive climate, let's create a classroom where everyone has access to high-quality supplies and no one controls supplies that are off-limits to others. The idea is to have community supplies only. All supplies are kept in community bins for everyone to use. If students and parents want to bring in other supplies for the whole class, they're welcome to. If students want to have their own special supplies that not everyone can share, they can keep those at home.

Make sure to communicate with parents so they know why you're using a community supply system. You may even want to communicate your approach to supplies in your welcome letter to students and families at the end of their fourth grade year, if a class list is available then, or over the summer. Some parents might be confused and even upset if there isn't a list of supplies to get for their child, but I've found that parents are very understanding if we explain our goals for having community supplies: building a strong community, making sure all students have access to high-quality supplies, and helping children learn how to share and cooperate.

Easy Access

Fifth graders are capable of great independence in the classroom. They should be able to get to the supplies that they need when they need them. For supplies to be easy to access, they should be:

- **Placed logically.** It makes sense to put crayons, pens, markers, and colored pencils all in the same areas; fraction puzzles, base ten blocks, color tiles, and pattern blocks on the same set of shelves; pipe cleaners, Wikki Stix, and craft sticks all together; and cleaning supplies near the sink. When we place supplies in areas that make sense, it's easier for students to find them when they need them.

- **Easy to see.** I remember once scavenging an old, unused, metal storage closet from the boiler room of my school. It was tall and deep and had doors to keep things looking neat. I carefully arranged lots of art supplies in the cabinet: paints, brushes, glitter, craft sticks, little pom-poms, and a box of fabric scraps. Then I introduced all of the materials to the class so that they could use them for various projects. But as the year went on, most of the supplies went unused. Because the doors were closed, the supplies weren't visible, so students didn't include them when planning their projects. Open shelves would have been a better way of organizing these supplies.

- **Easy to reach.** If students are supposed to be independent with supplies, they need to be able to reach them on their own. Not only did my salvaged cabinet hide the supplies, but it was also too tall and too deep for some students. Even if they could have seen the clay, they couldn't have reached it independently. With some students sprouting up in height, it might be tempting to count on taller students to help out shorter ones. Consider, though, that some students may be really sensitive about being shorter. Having to ask for help to reach supplies would likely cause embarrassment. Some may choose not to use the supplies rather than ask for help.

Great Fifth Grade Supplies

The following table shows examples of supplies to have in a fifth grade classroom, along with quantities for selected supplies. This is not meant to be an exhaustive list, but rather a starting point. Although the supplies are grouped by category, clearly many materials could fit in multiple categories.

Good Supplies for a Fifth Grade Classroom

Category	Early in the Year	Later in the Year	Sample Quantities
Art, social studies, projects	■ Crayons ■ Colored pencils ■ Markers (thin and thick) ■ Drawing paper ■ Construction paper ■ Magazines (for cutting from) ■ Various fabrics ■ Craft sticks ■ Glitter ■ Wikki Stix ■ Glue ■ Tape	■ Calligraphy pens ■ Wax pencils ■ Oil pastels ■ Paints ■ Oak tag ■ Stencils ■ Modeling clay ■ Hot glue gun ■ Colored tissue paper ■ Wire ■ Beads ■ Pipe cleaners	■ Scissors—one pair for every two students ■ Glue—one bottle for every two students ■ Markers, crayons, colored pencils—an ample supply for each table or desk cluster ■ Modeling clay—various colors (enough so that everyone can use some at the same time)
Literacy	■ Books, both fiction and nonfiction, multiple genres ■ Sticky notes ■ Paper for rough and final drafts ■ Pens, pencils ■ Highlighters ■ Staplers ■ Writing journals ■ Clipboards	■ Books (new genres; keep cycling in new books throughout the year) ■ Note cards ■ Binders ■ Clear plastic portfolio sleeves ■ Book binder	■ Books—a wide assortment, many in multiple copies ■ Pens, pencils—several dozen of each ■ Book binder—one for the class (teach students how to use it)

Good Supplies for a Fifth Grade Classroom

Category	Early in the Year	Later in the Year	Sample Quantities
Math	■ Rulers ■ Calculators ■ Base ten blocks ■ Protractors ■ Compasses ■ Graph paper ■ Variety of math games ■ Fraction puzzles	■ Tangrams ■ Tape measures ■ Sudoku puzzles ■ Cuisenaire rods ■ New math games ■ Coordinate geometry puzzles	■ Rulers, protractors, calculators—one for every student ■ Base ten blocks, Tangrams, Cuisenaire rods—large containers for small groups
Science	■ Science notebooks ■ Connex, Legos ■ Magnifying glasses ■ Rocks and minerals kits ■ Microscopes	■ Field guides ■ Human body puzzles, skeletons, and books ■ Other hands-on materials that match your curricula	■ Enough for partners or small groups ■ One science notebook per student
Recess (indoor and outdoor)	■ Math/logic games ■ Literacy games ■ Trivia books (also good for when the class is lined up waiting to go to lunch or assembly) ■ Jump ropes ■ Playground ball, football, basketball	■ Jigsaw puzzles ■ Mad Libs ■ Board games (quick ones such as Boggle and Yahtzee) ■ Computer games ■ Fun websites ■ Snow brick makers ■ Sidewalk chalk	■ When supplies are limited, such as with playground balls and computers, consider a rotating sign-out system so all students have a chance to use them.

See the appendix (pages 113–117) for favorite books, board games, and websites for fifth graders.

Technology

Depending on the resources available in your school, various kinds of technology can play an important role in your teaching. It's amazing what fifth graders can do with technology when given the proper structure and guidance. They can build websites, make movies, create podcasts, build PowerPoint presentations, and so much more. Still, technology resources can present challenges in the classroom and deserve special thought and attention.

■ **Use technology with purpose.** Be careful not to overuse technology. For example, interactive whiteboards are a wonderful tool, but they should be used only when doing so enhances the quality of instruction. If using an easel and chart paper would be easier and more effective for a class brainstorming session, then that's the tool to use.

Learn More about Classroom Setup at www.responsiveclassroom.org

Classroom Spaces That Work by Marlynn K. Clayton (Northeast Foundation for Children, 2001).

■ **Consider accessibility issues.** For instance, a child who uses a wheelchair might need certain accommodations when working at a computer station. Work with the experts in your school to ensure that every child can access the technology resources you plan to use.

■ **Allow students to teach each other.** Children are fully capable of exploring new technologies and teaching each other how to use them. Well-meaning teachers can actually get in the way by overexplaining or creating dull, step-by-step explorations of websites or software programs. Sometimes the best thing we can do is introduce the new technology, set a few simple guidelines and challenges or goals for students, and then get out of their way (while keeping an eye out for any unsafe or inappropriate use).

■ **Monitor technology use.** A great advantage of using technology with fifth graders is that they know so much. A great challenge of using technology with fifth graders is that they know so much! Though quite adept at navigating technology, fifth graders still need support and close supervision. Know your school's policy on appropriate technology use, teach it to your students, and stay vigilant.

Classroom Displays

Classroom displays serve many important purposes. They give students information and reminders about social and academic routines. They showcase and highlight work that students are doing, which increases students' sense of accomplishment and ownership of the classroom. Displays also enable parents, colleagues, and other visitors to "read" the walls and get a sense of all the work that's happening in the classroom.

Here are some ideas for student-centered classroom displays:

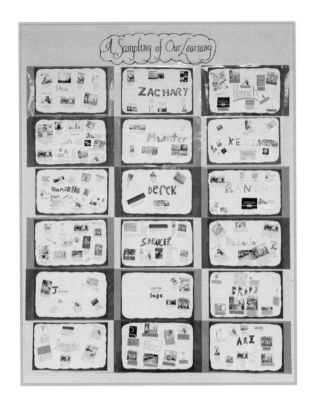

Student Work

It can't be overstated: Students' work needs to be displayed in the classroom. Displaying their work reinforces many important messages that we want to convey to students: We're proud of the work we do. We're working together to build a community of learners. We care about what we're learning. Our ideas and our work have value.

When displaying student work, keep the following points in mind:

■ **All students' work should be displayed.** Although we certainly can't (and shouldn't) display every piece of work that students do, every student should have at least one piece of work on display at any given time in the classroom. By doing so, we're telling students that each one of them is a valued member of the class and that everyone's work and learning is important. One caution: Aim for a reasonable balance in how many items each student has displayed. If, for example, a few students regularly have many displays posted while the rest of the class only has one or two, some hard feelings may result and you may send the wrong message to the class.

■ **Not all students need to have the same work displayed.** When I first started teaching, I tended to create a bulletin board that focused on a theme (such as tessellations in geometry) and had every student represented in the display. The problem was that twenty-five tessellation designs took up so much room that we could have only one or two bulletin boards at a time. As an alternative, consider creating display areas that showcase various topics and projects going on in the class. For example, some students might post poems they've written, others could post sample tessellations, still others could display character maps from the current read-aloud, and so on. This way, students will have many visual reminders of the multiple learning topics they're involved with.

■ **Display in-process work as well as finished products.** We often say to students that the process of learning is just as important as the product. We encourage them to take risks and make mistakes. We stress the importance of revising and editing. One way we can reinforce these messages is to display in-process work, just as we do with finished products. For example, post sample rough draft pages from students' writing, with all of the glorious cross-outs, misspelled words, and scribbles to show their thinking and effort. (Remember to get students' okay first before posting in-process work.)

■ **Let students help choose what to display.** When we allow students to choose some of their work to display in the room, we give them a greater degree of voice and empowerment. They need to carefully consider which pieces they're most proud of or which pieces accurately demonstrate their thinking and work. Fifth graders appreciate this level of trust and independence, and it helps them develop a greater sense of responsibility about their work.

Rules and Routines

Fifth graders benefit from visual reminders of classroom rules and daily routines. In the next chapter, we'll explore how to create and practice effective routines in fifth grade. For now, it's enough to know that although fifth graders are on the older end of the elementary school spectrum, they still need reminders about procedures for transitioning into the classroom in the morning, packing up at the end of the day, and other daily routines.

Anchor Charts

As we teach lessons, we introduce a lot of new information and skills all at once. Anchor charts are simple posters and charts that remind students of key information or academic skills that they're currently working on. Anchor charts should reflect the current content of the classroom—which means we should regularly replace or update them.

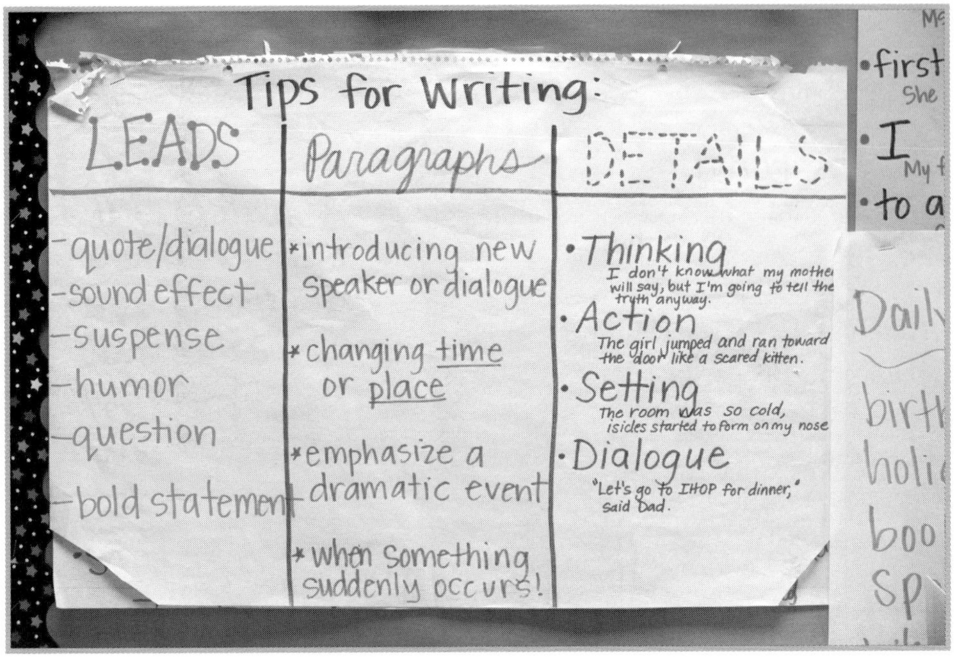

Tips for Writing:

LEADS	Paragraphs	DETAILS
-quote/dialogue -sound effect -suspense -humor -question -bold statement	*introducing new speaker or dialogue *changing time or place *emphasize a dramatic event *when something suddenly occurs!	•Thinking I don't know what my mother will say, but I'm going to tell the truth anyway. •Action The girl jumped and ran toward the door like a scared kitten. •Setting The room was so cold, isicles started to form on my nose •Dialogue "Let's go to IHOP for dinner," said Dad.

I visited a fantastic fifth grade classroom in a Boston public school recently. Here are the titles of the anchor charts in that classroom:

■ Ways We Choose Books

■ Expository Text Features

■ Evidence of Having Read Carefully

■ Word Wall

■ Writer's Club Guidelines

■ Relationships Among Quadrilaterals

■ Observations About Perimeter and Area

■ Breaking Apart One Number

■ Breaking Apart Two Numbers

■ Ways to Describe Triangles

■ Landforms Vocabulary

Each anchor chart provided key information that could help students do high-quality work. Taken together, the charts also were a daily reminder to the students of all that they were learning, which helped them feel competent and engaged with the classroom work. In deciding what anchor charts to display, keep the learning goals in mind.

Closing Thoughts

The day before school started one year, my principal popped her head through the classroom doorway and said, "Mike, this doesn't look like a classroom. It looks like a place where people come to do work." It was one of the nicest compliments I've ever received about a classroom. Indeed, our goal in setting up a classroom is to create a place where students can learn and do great work. When we take the time to purposefully plan a classroom—with fifth graders' common characteristics and needs in mind—they'll feel more comfortable, independent, and industrious throughout the school day and year.

CHAPTER 2

Schedules and Routines

In the weeks leading up to my first year of teaching, I focused mostly on two things. First, I had to get the physical layout of the room set. I inherited a classroom from a teacher who, over the course of twenty years, had accumulated multiple textbooks, curricular materials, trade books, reams of paper, and other supplies. I needed to sort through everything and decide what to keep and how best to arrange the room (which we discussed in Chapter 1).

My other focus was on the curriculum I was about to teach. I knew that I wanted to use a workshop approach to reading and writing, so I needed to gather enough books for a class library and have notebooks ready for writing. I also spent time looking over and getting ready to teach the first units in science, social studies, and math. By the first day of school, I felt pretty ready.

The things I neglected to focus on, however, were the schedules and routines of the classroom. That was a mistake! As I was soon to learn, a daily schedule is like the skeleton of the classroom—it supports everything else that happens throughout the day. And if the schedule is the skeleton of the classroom, then routines are its lifeblood. Students enter the classroom and put away backpacks and homework. They greet friends and check the schedule. Later in the day, they transition from one subject to another, from recess to lunch, and from lunch back into the classroom, with these routine activities sustaining the ebb and flow of life in the room.

Math, science, literacy, music, physical education, and all the other subjects demand much of our attention when teaching fifth graders. Yet, because schedules and routines have such a huge impact on students' learning, we need to deliberately plan and teach them, just as we plan and teach academic content.

33

Life in our classrooms can be frustrating and inefficient. Or it can be calm and orderly, giving fifth graders a sense of stability and leading them to productive learning. The difference is in how we set up schedules and routines and teach them to students. This chapter will give you effective ways to set up schedules and routines with fifth graders in mind. You'll also learn a great way to teach routines. And you'll get ideas that will enable the school day to flow smoothly for students—and for you.

Scheduling

As you begin to craft your schedule, you'll find that certain things may already be established. For example, the midday break for recess and lunch will probably be set, as will the specials schedule for the week (art, music, physical education, library, computer, and so on).

You'll also discover that some parts of the schedule may be somewhat flexible. For example, the reading specialist may approach you to find out when she can come into your classroom to support four students as they read. This teacher is likely trying to coordinate her time with other teachers in the building as well. So you may want to collaborate with the other fifth grade teachers to plan times that work well for everyone—adjusting them as needed throughout the year—to ensure that students get the reading support they need while minimizing disruptions.

Then there will be other times of the day that are completely flexible. For example, you may be able to choose when a science block can take place. Our goal should be to make the best use of what flexibility we do have to create classroom schedules that are most conducive to joyful and challenging learning for students.

Think about Fifth Graders' Needs

Fifth graders are social. Fifth graders are growing. Fifth graders can go with the flow. These are just a few of their common characteristics to keep in mind as you plan a daily schedule. Here are some specific suggestions:

■ **Provide frequent breaks.** Fifth graders may struggle if they have to wait until the middle of the day for one long recess and lunch break. Instead, include a couple of short breaks throughout the day to give them multiple chances to connect with friends, get some physical movement, and reenergize for more learning.

■ **Alternate silent and interactive periods of the day.** If possible, avoid having back-to-back learning activities that require students to work silently on their own. Instead, try to alternate periods of quiet solo work with more interactive learning time. For example, after students have read silently during reading workshop, they'll appreciate engaging in a science project where they get to chat as they work.

■ **Build in a little social time for transitions.** I've caught myself challenging students to transition from one subject to the next without talking. In fifth grade, we might as well challenge them to not breathe! If we tell students they should put away their math work and get out their social studies research folders without talking to one another, we're going to be fighting a losing battle all year. Instead, build in an extra minute or two for students to talk as they transition. Use interactive modeling (see pages 37–41) to teach them how to keep conversations brief and how to refocus as they move on to the next activity.

■ **Make time to eat.** Whether you plan official snack times or allow students to eat throughout the day, be sure to consider this important aspect of the day. Some students will come to school hungry, not having had enough (or any) breakfast. Most students will need to eat a couple of times during the school day,

---

Easing the Recess-to-Classroom Transition

■ **Recess first.** Exercising and then eating fits how children's (and adults') bodies naturally work. When physical needs are met, behavior generally improves. If your school schedules lunch first, you may want to suggest trying it the other way around.

■ **Quiet time.** Consider having ten to fifteen minutes of silent, independent work time after students enter the room from recess and lunch. They can read, draw, catch up on homework, or work on a math or word puzzle. This quiet time helps children shift gears.

■ **Read-aloud.** Listening to a good book together right after recess and lunch can ease any ruffled feelings and help the group settle into the afternoon. See the appendix (pages 113–117) for some favorite fifth grade read-alouds.

in addition to their lunch period, to keep their energy high for learning. Growing and learning take a lot of energy, and we need to make sure students stay fueled up.

■ **Talk with colleagues and school leaders about the frequency of changing classes.** Fifth grade often marks the year when students start changing classes. Students can benefit by experiencing such changes (for example, when changing teachers for math and science). However, too many changes can be difficult for students to adjust to socially and emotionally; they can also be very challenging for teachers to manage. If your school's fifth graders are changing classes a lot, talk with other teachers and school leaders about finding a productive balance.

The following schedules give you two possible starting points for building your own schedule.

Two Ideal Schedules

Time	Activity		Time	Activity
8:30–8:40	Arrival Routine		8:30–8:40	Arrival Routine
8:40–9:00	Morning Meeting		8:40–9:05	Morning Meeting
9:00–9:55	Math		9:05–10:05	Science
9:55–10:05	Snack Break		10:05–10:20	Recess
10:05–11:05	Reading Workshop		10:20–11:30	Literacy*
11:05–12:00	Social Studies		11:30–12:30	Special
12:00–12:45	Recess and Lunch		12:30–1:15	Recess and Lunch
12:45–1:05	Read-aloud		1:15–2:15	Math
1:05–1:45	Writing Workshop		2:15–3:00	Social Studies*
1:45–1:55	Snack Break		3:00–3:20	Read-aloud
1:55–2:35	Science or Social Studies		3:20–3:30	Dismissal Routine
2:35–3:20	Special		* Students may eat while working during these periods.	
3:20–3:30	Dismissal Routine			

Teaching Classroom Routines

We might assume that because fifth graders have been going to school for so long, they already know what to do on the first day of their new school year with us. That's what I thought when I first started teaching fifth grade: Weren't these students old enough to know, for example, how to line up quietly without a lot of explanation? But in fact, all elementary students, including those in fifth grade, need to be taught how to line up. And how to raise their hand when they have a question, how to turn in their homework, and so on. After all, students can forget about school routines over the long summer. They probably also had different teachers the previous year, each of whom likely had different expectations and routines.

Certainly, fifth graders will know more than younger grade children, and we should honor this knowledge. But when we take the time to teach students the routines of this classroom, for this year, they're more likely to be comfortable and successful. As a result, the learning environment will be more relaxed and efficient. Teaching classroom routines is one of our most important jobs with fifth grade students, especially at the beginning of the school year.

Use Interactive Modeling to Teach Routines

Before we get into which classroom skills and routines are most important to teach in fifth grade, let's first look at how to teach skills and routines. A simple and effective way is to use interactive modeling. This technique gives students the opportunity to think about, observe, discuss, and practice the skills needed to perform classroom routines independently. The table on the next page shows what the steps of interactive modeling might look and sound like if you were teaching students how to put calculators back in the class storage bin.

Interactive Modeling: Putting Away Calculators

Steps to Follow	Might Sound/Look Like
1 Describe a positive behavior you will model.	"After we use the calculators, we need to put them away carefully so they'll stay in good condition throughout the year. I'm going to model that. Watch what I do."
2 Model the behavior.	Place the calculator in the bin, just the way you want students to do it. You don't need to say anything or narrate what you're doing. Describing your actions can make it harder for students to focus on them.
3 Ask students what they noticed.	"What were some ways I was careful as I put away my calculator?" Students might say, "You put it in gently" or "You placed it to the side of the container so more can fit in."
4 Ask student volunteers to model the same behavior.	"Let's have a couple of you give it a try. Who would like to show us how to put a calculator away carefully?"
5 Ask students what they noticed. (Repeat steps 4 and 5 as needed.)	"What were some ways that Cam, Tonya, and Maci were careful as they put their calculators in the bin?" Students name specific behaviors that were demonstrated.
6 Have the class practice.	"Now it's time for the rest of you to try. I'll call you up a few at a time and you can put your calculators away."
7 Provide feedback.	"Right on! These calculators are all stacked neatly in the bin. They were also placed there carefully. If we put calculators away like this, they'll last us all year."

Keys to Successful Interactive Modeling

CLEARLY ARTICULATE ROUTINES FOR YOURSELF

An important first step of modeling something well for students is to clearly articulate for ourselves what the routine should look like. I remember once saying to a class of students that they needed to "be quiet" during transitions within the classroom. As students were moving about, some students were talking with each other, some were whispering, and some weren't making any sound at all. As some students' voices started to get louder, I tried reminding them to keep their voices down, but I also realized that I wasn't sure myself how loud their voices should be. If I wasn't sure, how could they be? I decided I needed to reteach this routine, and I had to start by figuring out exactly what voice level would be okay so that I could model this for students.

MAKE SURE EXPECTATIONS ARE REALISTIC

Be careful about setting standards that are too high. In the previous example, to require fifth graders to transition silently in the classroom is probably unrealistic. Can they do it? Sure. But the amount of time and energy that will be spent trying to enforce silent transitions will likely lead to constant frustration for both teachers and students. It's even hard for adults to follow a "be silent" rule. And why should fifth graders have to be silent anyway? Isn't the goal of being quiet to make sure that other students can stay focused and to preserve a calm environment? If that's the goal, teach students how to whisper or talk quietly so that they can chat with friends while not disturbing others as they move about the classroom.

BE CONSISTENT

Once you've modeled and practiced routines that are realistic and age-appropriate, make sure to hold students accountable for them. If students are allowed to whisper while walking, yet three students are chatting and laughing in regular voices, redirect them to get them back on track. If many students are having trouble with an expected behavior, you may want to repeat the interactive modeling process for that behavior. When we consistently hold students accountable for an expected level of behavior, they feel safe and secure, knowing that there are limits.

One of the key principles of interactive modeling is to not assume that students already know how the classroom routines will work. Yet, don't assume that they know nothing. In fact, fifth graders begin the year with a considerable amount of school experience. You can draw on this as you model and practice key routines, reinforcing for students that they're older and more competent, while also teaching them specific, positive behaviors. For example, when modeling how to walk quietly, you might say, "What are some strategies that you use to remind yourself to stay quiet as you walk?" Allowing students to share their ideas and expertise is both empowering and affirming.

PROVIDE ONGOING REINFORCEMENT AND REMINDING

Students will need support as they continue to practice the behaviors you taught. When the class does well, reinforce the positive behavior: "That trip from our classroom to the art room was spot-on. People were whispering so that kids in other classes could stay focused on learning. That's just the way it should sound!"

If a routine has been especially tough for a particular student, you might pull that child aside for a private reinforcement when he or she does well: "Jenny, I know that you've been working at keeping your voice quiet as we walk in the halls. Did you notice

---

Transitioning to Greater Independence

Something that often happens in fifth grade (especially if fifth grade is the highest grade in the school) is that we start to let behavior standards slip. Maybe we want to give fifth graders more independence, so we send them off to navigate the school day without providing enough support or guidance.

Regardless of the reason, we must insist on high standards of behavior for fifth graders. We need to let them be more independent than they were in the lower grades, but still teach them appropriate behaviors and keep a watchful eye and ear. For example, in middle school, these children will be traveling the halls by themselves, not with their teachers.

So we can start to empower them by gradually giving them more responsibility in this area: "You're all old enough to start walking in the halls without having to go in a line everywhere. Next year, in the middle school, you'll need to get from class to class without adults walking you there. We're going to start practicing a new routine for walking in the hallway this week. What are some things you'll need to keep in mind so that you're taking care of yourselves and others when I'm not there?"

In this way, as the school year progresses, you can maintain high expectations, but start to shift those expectations, helping fifth graders become more independent, responsible, and self-disciplined.

40

how well you just did that? You even kept your voice to a whisper when Ms. Rodriguez greeted you as we passed the office!"

Watch how students are doing and offer quick refreshers when needed: "Yesterday, I noticed that our voices were starting to get very loud as we got close to the gym. Remember to keep using soft voices until we're at our destination." Model the routine again if necessary.

Key Routines to Teach

Transitioning within the classroom and walking in the hallways are just some of the many skills and routines to teach and practice with students. The following sections outline other key categories of routines to teach, including more on transitions. When you take the time to teach students the appropriate times and ways to sharpen pencils, use the bathroom, move chairs about the room, and carry out other classroom routines, the school day runs more smoothly. And in so doing, you're creating an environment that allows for great learning.

SIGNALS FOR ATTENTION

Signals seem so basic, yet they're profoundly important. If students are to move smoothly throughout the school day, you need to set up respectful and efficient ways of getting their attention. Students also need to know how to get your attention in respectful and efficient ways as they work and play.

Effective Use of Signals

■ **Use signals that can work in a variety of settings.** Complex or multiple signals can lead to inconsistent responses.

■ **Expect a quick, not an instantaneous, response.** You don't need to demand immediate attention, which can feel disrespectful to students and create power struggles. Instead, give students about 15 seconds to stop what they're doing before they respond.

■ **Wait until every student responds to the signal before you speak.** Don't speak until everyone is quiet. Be consistent: Mean what you say and say what you mean.

The best signals are simple visual and auditory ones. When students see or hear the signal, they complete their work or conversations within fifteen seconds or so, turn their bodies toward the person who gave the signal, and remain quiet. The consistent use of signals such as the following will help the classroom become a calm, respectful learning environment.

■ **Visual signal.** Simply raising your hand and waiting until all students are listening is an incredibly effective signal to use with fifth graders. Teach students that when they see your raised hand, they quickly wrap up their conversations and work, get quiet, and look at you, so that you can address the class.

■ **Auditory signal.** A raised hand won't work if students are so engrossed in their work that no one is looking at you. So use a chime, bell, rain stick, or some other pleasant-sounding instrument to get the attention of the group in these instances. As with the visual signal, model and practice exactly what students should do to follow this signal, and then hold students to that standard. Remind or redirect them, or repeat the interactive modeling, as needed.

■ **Student signal.** How should students get your attention when they have a question or need help? What if they raise their hand and you don't see it? What if they need help but you're working with another group? Make sure students know how to get your attention in respectful ways. Model and practice these routines, and then stick to them. For example, students might sign up on a conference board when they need to meet with you, but you're busy helping someone else. One teacher I know has students put something (a bright piece of paper or card) on the table near where they're working to signal that they need help.

Also be sure to tell students that it is always OK for them to come directly over to you if they're having an emergency, rather than use a signal. Teach and model how to come quickly and calmly over to you during these times.

BEGINNING OF THE DAY

Consider the many tasks that children have to do to start off their school day: get breakfast in the cafeteria, fill out their lunch ticket, get a note from home signed in the office, return a library book, hang up their backpack and coat, pass in their homework, and read the morning message and follow its directions. When you think about all the details involved in accomplishing these tasks efficiently, it's no wonder that students need some guidance.

To help students get off to a smooth start and be prepared for learning, try working with the class to list all the tasks that they need to do as they start the school day. Decide if some tasks can be moved to less hectic times of the day. Next, use interactive modeling to teach students the most challenging tasks (or reteach the ones they're having the most trouble with). Finally, make and post anchor charts of the morning tasks to serve as reminders. When students know what to do (and how to do it), everyone will have a much better start to the day!

43

MORNING ROUTINE
Remember to ...

✓ Hang up coats.

✓ Take snacks out of backpacks.

✓ Pass in homework.

✓ Pass in any notes from home.

✓ Do morning errands.

✓ Use the bathroom.

✓ Fill out lunch ticket.

✓ Read morning message.

✓ Join in meeting area for morning meeting.

Sample Start-of-Day Anchor Chart

RECESS AND LUNCH

The midday break for recess and lunch can be a great time for students to connect with friends, get a little exercise, play some games, and recharge their batteries for an afternoon of learning. Unfortunately, it can also be a time of day marked by teasing, exclusion, and confusing guidelines and rules. You can help ensure that this time of day goes well for students by focusing on these key routines:

- How to fill out a lunch ticket

- Where to put lunch boxes during recess

- How to know whether to bring a coat outside

- What to do if someone gets hurt on the playground

- How to line up when recess is over

- How to move safely and considerately through the lunch line

- How to know where to sit in the cafeteria

- How to join a lunch table and how to welcome someone to the lunch table

- How to reenter the classroom for the afternoon

Use interactive modeling to teach these routines, and make anchor charts and post them as reminders for students. For more on recess and lunch, see Chapter 3, "Building Community," pages 66–69.

44

RECESS & LUNCH ROUTINE

Remember to ...

✓ Clean work space.

✓ Get lunch.

✓ Sign out recess equipment.

✓ Get coat.

✓ Walk quietly in halls.

Sample Recess/Lunch Anchor Chart

END OF THE DAY

By the time the end of the day rolls around, both fifth graders and teachers may be pretty wiped out. This is also a time of day when teachers and students are usually thinking about vastly different things. While teachers are pressing to squeeze as much learning out of the last lesson of the day as possible, students are starting to think about what happens after school. In the rush, teachers may forget to provide students with the time and support they need to have a productive and relaxed end of the day.

As you did for the beginning-of-school tasks, brainstorm a list of end-of-day tasks with your students. Estimate how much time each task will take. Once you've totaled up these times, you'll know how long students need to get ready at the end of the day. Remember to see if some tasks can

Ending the Day with a Closing Circle

A closing circle (or closing meeting) can be a calming and focused way to close the school day. You can have the class gather for a quiet reflection or for a relaxed game. Here are a few other ideas for a closing circle:

■ **Sharing and reflecting.** Students chat with a partner or take turns in an "around-the-circle" share, discussing what they learned or enjoyed about school that day.

■ **Playing a game or singing.** Invite students to play a math or spelling game or sing a favorite song.

Learn More about Closing Circles at www.responsiveclassroom.org

"Closing Circle," *Responsive Classroom Newsletter*, February 2011. Also, search on the term "closing circle" for more information.

45

be moved to other times of the day. Then, teach students the routines they'll need to follow to complete their end-of-day tasks, using interactive modeling. Post anchor charts as reminders, too.

To further ensure that you'll avoid an end-of-day scramble and finish on a positive note, make a closing circle part of your classroom routine. A closing circle allows students and teachers to end the day in fun, relaxing, and reflective ways. About ten minutes before dismissal, stop your lesson, gather the children in the meeting spot, and wind down together.

TRANSITIONS

"Okay, everyone. Put away your math work and get ready for recess." Sounds simple enough, right? Not quite! To transition from math to recess, students need to complete many steps, from putting away their work to lining up to go outside. Transitioning from one subject to the next can involve multiple steps, too.

END-OF-DAY ROUTINE
Remember to ...

✓ Pack up homework.

✓ Get coat, hat, etc.

✓ Do afternoon tasks (clean up, put away supplies).

✓ Think about afterschool activities.

✓ Gather for closing circle.

Sample End-of-Day Anchor Chart

We may feel pressured to pack as much learning time as we can into every work period, so it's easy to hurry transitions. But when we do, the classroom climate can feel rushed and chaotic. By creating transitions that allow enough time, structure, and support, we can ensure that these times of the day are calm and reassuring for students while giving them the mental space to actually learn more in the long run.

Use interactive modeling to teach students how to transition well. Here are some of the transition behaviors you'll want to model and practice with students:

❖ Putting work away

❖ Getting a drink of water

❖ Using the bathroom

❖ Moving from meeting area to desks (and vice versa)

❖ Lining up

In addition, here are a few other things you can do to set students up for successful transitions:

■ **Visual reminders.** For complicated, multistep transitions, students benefit from having anchor charts listing the essential steps (similar to the ones for the start of the day, page 43; recess and lunch, page 44; and the end of the day, page 46). Create these charts with your class by brainstorming what they need to remember during these times. When they're involved in making the charts, students will be more likely to use them throughout the day.

■ **Verbal reminders.** Quick verbal reminders help keep students on track. Consider how some of the following reminders might set students up for success:

Learn More about Schedules and Routines at
www.responsiveclassroom.org

The First Six Weeks of School by Paula Denton and Roxann Kriete (Northeast Foundation for Children, 2000).

❖ "We're heading to PE. Make sure you have your sneakers."

❖ "That was a great writing share. We're about to transition to math. What are some things we need to do as we move from writing to math?"

❖ "Yesterday, quite a few people forgot to bring their notebook to the circle for our whole-group lesson. Let's all work on remembering that for this afternoon's lesson."

❖ "It's time to put away art supplies and get ready for snack. Let's list some things we need to remember to do."

■ **Revisit and remodel.** You may find as the year goes on that a particular transition just isn't working. If several students are having a hard time with the same transition, the problem likely lies with the transition, not the students. Have a short class meeting and see what's going on: "I've noticed that the end of the day is often feeling very rushed and that many people are having a hard time staying calm. Let's share some ideas about why that's happening and what we can do to make it better."

ACADEMIC ROUTINES

Up to this point, we've explored various routines that students need to learn so that they can navigate the school day. We need to pay the same kind of attention to the academic routines of the day. Here are a few key academic routines to model and practice with fifth graders:

- ❖ Sharing a piece of writing with a partner
- ❖ Offering positive feedback to a partner
- ❖ Logging on to school computers
- ❖ Searching for useful Internet sites
- ❖ Using calculators to check work
- ❖ Taking digital photos of work samples for portfolios
- ❖ Reading aloud to book buddies
- ❖ Listening closely during read-alouds

With so many academic routines to teach, it can be hard to figure out which ones to teach first. Here's one approach for deciding: As you plan each lesson and activity, take a quick, mental walk through the activity from the perspective of students in the classroom. What will each student need to do as a part of the work you're assigning? What might they already know how to do? What might they struggle with? Keeping a "student's-eye view" of the classroom often points to the academic routines and structures that students will need guidance and support with.

Learn More about Interactive Modeling and Academic Routines at www.responsiveclassroom.org

Learning Through Academic Choice by Paula Denton, EdD (Northeast Foundation for Children, 2005).

EMERGENCIES

Throughout the year, your school will likely practice several emergency drills: fire, bus evacuation, lockdown, and others. It's a good idea to walk through these procedures with your students before the school practices them as a whole. This is especially important for anxious students, who can get very nervous during these kinds of drills. In fact, modeling and practicing just what to do before there are hundreds of other students involved can help calm everyone's nerves. It can also enable fifth graders to serve as appropriate role models for younger students.

What about when there's a classroom emergency, such as a student who has a bloody nose or gets sick? Make sure classroom routines are in place for these times and practice them in advance. For example:

- ❖ If students are working independently, they keep working.

- ❖ If you're in the middle of a lesson or all together in the meeting area, students move to their seats and find something to read.

- ❖ If you need to step out of the classroom, a student whom you've previously designated to act as messenger alerts the next-door teacher.

- ❖ A student who feels sick and needs to see the school nurse fills out a pass (if required) that you sign.

OTHER ROUTINES

Depending on the classroom setup and students' needs, you may also want to use interactive modeling to teach routines for bathroom breaks, daily meetings, and read-alouds, and to teach social skills such as greeting people in respectful, friendly ways. What other routines do your students need to learn? Think about other parts of the day that might be confusing or challenging for students and how you can use interactive modeling to help set them up for success.

Closing Thoughts

One of the most exciting aspects of teaching fifth grade is that students are able to handle more (and more challenging) content than in the lower elementary grades. It can be tempting, then, for fifth grade teachers to focus almost exclusively on teaching academic content while hoping fifth graders can figure out most routines by themselves. However, as a colleague of mine likes to say, "Hope is not a classroom management strategy!"

Investing time in setting up effective schedules and in teaching students key routines is still wise. It will pay huge dividends, especially later in the year when fifth graders can become more independent. Students will feel comfortable and safe. They'll feel more confident in taking positive academic risks, and they'll be more likely to do high-quality project work and be more responsible, self-motivated learners.

CHAPTER 3

Building Community

In many schools, fifth grade is when academics get much more intense. Homework loads increase. Greater expectations for learning content may be placed on students throughout the school day and year. We often expect fifth graders to take on large projects, which involve more responsibility and more independence than ever before. In light of these increased academic demands, we might assume that community building should take a back seat.

But at the same time as academic demands on them are increasing, many fifth graders are entering a new phase of intense social development. Peer relationships are taking on greater importance. Students are paying more attention to friendships. Interest in hairstyles and clothing fads seems to blossom. Cliques and teasing may increase. How should teachers manage all of this? If we can keep students busy, the thinking sometimes goes, perhaps we can diminish their focus on social interactions and increase their engagement in academics.

In fact, however, acknowledging fifth graders' need for social interaction and intentionally working on community building actually do more to help students thrive academically. If we neglect to build safe and positive communities, snide comments might fly when someone gets a math problem wrong. Students may trade insults or disengage during writing conferences. We might see eyes rolling during oral presentations. And as a result, students' academic and social development suffers.

On the other hand, when we build a strong community in which empathy and trust are the norm, students will be better able to listen during writing conferences and offer one another helpful advice. They'll more willingly ask questions and answer them honestly. And students will be more likely to

51

get excited about each others' work and be respectful and supportive class-mates. This is the kind of community that can make teaching fifth graders so rewarding and enjoyable! We should begin our community-building work on the very first day of school—and keep it front and center throughout the year.

Teacher Tone and Demeanor

Teachers have more impact on the climate and culture of the classroom than anyone else. When we demonstrate respect, inclusion, friendliness, good sportsmanship, and other prosocial qualities, we provide ongoing positive modeling for our students. As I travel, visiting classrooms all over the country, I see the power of positive teacher modeling reflected time and time again in the way children behave toward classmates and others in the learning community.

Consider the following scene: Four students are supposed to be working together to solve math problems, but instead they're chatting about the soccer game that two of them played in yesterday. The teacher needs to get the students back on track so they can finish their math work. So he approaches the students with an open posture, smiling, and speaks in a friendly, yet businesslike, tone. "I know yesterday's soccer game was exciting, but right now it's time to focus on your math work. Recess and lunch are coming up in thirty minutes. That would be a better time to talk about the game."

At times like these, and especially if we're tending to a lot of things in the room or feeling crunched for time, it's easy to slip and say things or use a tone of voice we'll later regret. But the importance of positive teacher language and body posture can't be overstated. Consider how you would feel if you were a student and a teacher was sarcastic or accusatory. How would this tone of voice likely affect your work? Would you be more or less eager to put positive energy into it? Might nearby students also feel bad about this interaction and get distracted from their work?

Learn More about Positive Teacher Language at www.responsiveclassroom.org

❖ Check out *The Power of Our Words* by Paula Denton, EdD (Northeast Foundation for Children, 2007).

❖ Search the *Responsive Classroom Newsletter* online.

Now think about the approach that the teacher in our example took. He redirected the group and helped them get back to work. He also affirmed their natural desire to talk about an exciting event and gave suggestions for another, more appropriate time to do so. Most importantly, his calm demeanor and respectful tone of voice set a calm mood and provided a model for how people are expected to treat each other in the classroom.

Here are some keys to using your teacher demeanor to help build a positive classroom climate:

- **Assume positive intentions.** Let students know that you believe that they want to be productive members of the classroom community through the words you use. For example: "We all want our classroom to be a friendly and caring place. What are some ideas you have for how we should talk or act during this math activity so that we're friendly and caring?"

- **Recognize positives.** Students need to know when they're doing something well. Give clear and simple statements to let students know when you see them behaving in positive ways. For example: "Nico, you're doing really well at listening to partners during reading shares. That helps them feel respected." "Congratulations, Maria—you just wrote two pages in your writers' notebook!" Even positive recognition can be very embarrassing for fifth graders if done publicly, so make sure you give this reinforcement in private, directly to the student. Doing so also helps you guard against recognizing one student to get other students on track.

- **Use inclusive language.** For instance, "we're going to work a bit more on our science projects today" makes the work sound more collaborative than "you're going to . . ." When addressing the class, use terms that include all students: "Okay, fifth graders, it's time to move to our circle." Avoid terms such as "boys and girls," which convey that the class is made up of separate groups.

53

Use humor, but avoid sarcasm. Fifth graders love to be playful, so telling funny stories about yourself to highlight a point or being playful during lessons helps students join together for a good laugh. We should never, however, use jokes that cut anyone down or use sarcasm, which can hurt students' feelings. Here's an example: At the end of a work period, the classroom is messy. We might say, "Oh . . . my . . . gosh. We've got some cleaning up to do," instead of saying, "Look at this room! Do you think I'm your personal cleaning service?" And whatever the purpose of your "teacher talks," keep them brief and take time to listen to what the children have to say.

Greetings

Maureen Manzo, a fifth grade teacher in Virginia, begins each school day the same way. She waits for students at the classroom doorway, ready with a handshake and a smile for each student.

"Good morning, Jamal! It's great to see you today!"

"Hi, Rosie! How are you doing this morning?"

"Good morning, David! How was your visit with your cousin last night?"

"Hey, Marisol! I'm glad you're back. Are you feeling better today? We missed you yesterday!"

Many teachers greet students in a similar way each morning. This simple act has many benefits. For one, it helps students start each day on a positive note. Having a friendly interaction with the children first thing in the morning can get us in a good mood, too. Also, you might be surprised by how much important information you can gather during this quick greeting. David is a bit tired. Rosie is happy and relaxed. Jamal is worried about his grandfather, who is ill. Marisol is anxious to learn what she missed in school.

For any child having a rough morning, a friendly greeting from the teacher can do a lot to make the classroom a "soft place to land." For all children, it can be reassuring to know that their teacher will be waiting at the door for them and that they can give her a quick heads-up on how they're doing. This simple connection each morning helps us set the tone for a positive and caring classroom community for the rest of the day.

In addition to our greeting of students, we can also teach students to greet one another and lead them in these greetings each day. The daily greeting is a simple but powerful practice that further strengthens the learning community. I start off each morning with a *Responsive Classroom* Morning Meeting. Each Morning Meeting begins with a simple greeting, which helps

students feel a sense of belonging and significance in the classroom. If you don't hold a morning meeting with your class, you could still have students greet each other every morning.

Here are some tips for setting up and running effective greetings in fifth grade:

■ **Gather the class in a circle.** Using a circle reinforces the sense of community we're trying to cultivate. Being able to see and be seen by everyone says "We're a team" and "Everyone is important."

■ **Simple is better.** Although there may be times when fanciful or complicated greetings might be appropriate, simple greetings are generally best. A handshake and a hello—while using each other's names and a friendly tone of voice—are the most important elements of a good greeting. Trying to do too much or make greetings feel like a game may make them feel less sincere. See "Some Good Fifth Grade Greetings" on the next page for ideas.

■ **Try whole-group greetings.** I've found that, perhaps due to their increasing sense of social relationships, some fifth graders, especially at the beginning of the year, feel pretty nervous when greeting someone while everyone else watches. So try some greetings where everyone greets a partner at the same time, or try a mix-and-mingle greeting where everyone has one minute to get up and greet several classmates. This can take the pressure off students and help them focus more on practicing the specific skills of giving and receiving friendly, sincere greetings.

Some Good Fifth Grade Greetings

■ **Have students partner with a neighbor in the circle.** Determine which partner will start. Then have partners greet each other in a friendly way.

■ **Greet several people nearby.** Divide the circle into small groups and have students greet each other within their group. Decide on the group size yourself, or let students decide.

■ **Mix and mingle.** Give students a minute or two to move around and greet several classmates. Challenge students to greet people they don't normally hang out with at recess or lunch. Remind students to take their time and make sure their greetings are sincere and meaningful.

■ **Category greeting.** Once students know each other well, challenge them to greet students who have a certain attribute. Split the class into two groups. You might begin by telling the first group to greet someone in the other group who likes art. Now give the other group a turn: "Greet someone in the other group who has a sibling in our school." Have the class brainstorm attributes, making sure that everyone will be included and that the attributes are appropriate.

■ **Greet and share.** To extend a simple greeting, have students greet another person and then talk about an assigned topic for a minute or two. Again, students might brainstorm topics together, or you might choose something related to that day's curriculum. For example: "Once you and your partner have greeted each other, talk about the science work we did yesterday with batteries. What are you thinking about trying today when you work with batteries again?"

Learn More about Greetings and Morning Meeting at www.responsiveclassroom.org

The Morning Meeting Book by Roxann Kriete (Northeast Foundation for Children, 2002).

99 Activities and Greetings: Great for Morning Meeting … and other meetings, too! by Melissa Correa-Connolly (Northeast Foundation for Children, 2004).

■ **Use interactive modeling.** Speaking of skills . . . we need to teach (and reteach) them. Interactive modeling is a great way to help students zero in on the specific attributes of a sincere greeting, such as turning toward the person you're greeting, politely asking his or her name if you forgot it, speaking in a friendly tone and using a firm handshake. Avoid giving students too much to think about at once when teaching these skills. Instead, focus on one or two skills at a time. For example, early in the year, begin by simply teaching them to say, "Good morning, [classmate's name]," without shaking hands. Handshakes, or moving around while greeting others, can be added later as students are ready to expand their skill set. See Chapter 2, "Schedules and Routines," pages 37–41, for more on interactive modeling.

■ **Be patient, be explicit.** At first, some students may feel that greetings are "little kid stuff." Don't let fifth graders off the hook so easily! Explain why it's important to greet others each day. I often say to students: "Learning how to greet others is an incredibly useful life skill. Some day, you're going to apply to colleges and for jobs. Knowing how to shake hands, make eye contact, and greet others in a respectful and friendly way can make a big difference in how well these important social interactions go. In the classroom, greetings are just as important. We're going to be working with each other all year long, so we need to develop a positive classroom climate that will help us do great work together."

Getting to Know Each Other

Since fifth graders will have to work together effectively all year long, they need to get to know each other so that they can start building a sense of trust in one another. Although many fifth graders may have been together in school for several years, we still need to make sure that all students know something about each of their classmates and have a chance to form positive connections. Otherwise, cliques are more likely to form as students cling to the friends they already have.

There are lots of great ways to help students get to know each other at the beginning of the school year. Here are a few ideas:

Personal Collages

Have students create a collage that helps them share interesting information about themselves with the rest of the class. They might include pictures of themselves playing sports or musical instruments, photos of their family or pets, or magazine cutouts of favorite animals. Students might also want to include drawings and writings about what's important to them, such as a hobby, a favorite book, a goal for the year, or something they hope to do further in the future. (Be sure to okay collages before they're finalized. You might be surprised by the pictures fifth graders choose to include.)

You can do lots of variations on the personal collage as well as some great follow-up activities once the collages are finished. For example:

■ **Family crest or family tree.** In one fifth grade class I visited, students created their own family crests by drawing pictures, writing words, and pasting photos of themselves in four categories: families, special skills and hobbies, favorite things, and school (or family) goals. Another class created family trees, also using drawings, photos, and writing. These family crests and family trees were posted proudly on a bulletin board for everyone to see. Both projects helped students share a bit about their families with their classmates.

■ **Class puzzle.** A colleague of mine had her fifth graders create their collages on huge puzzle pieces that she had cut out for them. Once all of the collages were finished, the class teamed up to fit all the puzzle pieces together. The teacher used this project as a starting place for class discussions about inclusion, teamwork, and cooperation.

■ **Class scavenger hunt.** Once collages are posted, create a class scavenger hunt designed to help students become more familiar with one another. Challenge students to find people they have connections with based on their collages. For example, see if students can find three different people who have younger brothers. A bonus of this kind of activity is that you, too, will get to know students better as you look through their collages while creating the scavenger hunt.

Fun Cooperative Projects

Another great way to help students get to know classmates and begin learning to work together is by doing a fun, and slightly challenging, cooperative project. Make sure you clearly explain the goals of this project to students: to have fun, to get to know each other better, and to learn how to work effectively as a team or partnership. For this first foray into team projects, choose topics and activities that aren't overly personal or too complicated. Here are a few suggestions:

■ **Hot air balloons.** This is one of my favorite classroom activities. When I taught fourth grade, I used it as a science project and saved it for the end of the year. When I moved to fifth grade, I decided to try it as a beginning-of-the-year project and found that it worked really well. Pair students up and lead them through the process of creating hot air balloons out of tissue paper (check out http://juniorballoonist.com and other websites for tips). Then gather together on the playground to launch the balloons. This is also an exciting event to share with families—it can give everyone a great early look at what fifth grade will be like!

Learn about Guided Discovery at www.responsiveclassroom.org

One way to help students gain skills and expertise with classroom materials is to use the *Responsive Classroom* process called Guided Discovery. This process, which focuses on observation, brainstorming, and exploratory play, is explained in more detail in *Learning Through Academic Choice* by Paula Denton, EdD (Northeast Foundation for Children, 2005).

■ **Class illustrations.** Have partners or small groups create illustrations of scenes from your first class read-aloud book. Post these illustrations on a bulletin board that shows the timeline of the book. You'll find great opportunities to talk about various story elements while also helping students learn how to share materials and plan and execute a unified design. Keep this time relaxing so students can chitchat as they work, building social connections. If you do this project again for more read-aloud books, rotate partners and small groups so that students get to work with other classmates.

■ **Exploring manipulatives and other materials.** You likely have some materials in math and science that students will use throughout the school year. At the beginning of the year, have students explore these materials in small groups. For example, challenge groups to make cool designs out of pattern blocks. Introduce the bin of Legos that will be used later in the year for work with simple machines and let students build with a partner. On a Friday afternoon, introduce several board games that will be in the indoor recess cupboard, put students in small groups, and have them try out the games. You'll be teaching students how to use and take care of classroom materials as well as giving them a chance to play and work together.

Simple Mini Field Trip

Is there a local park you could walk to for some community-building games or nature observations? How about a local business that might be interested in giving fifth graders a behind-the-scenes look at how it works? If so, consider taking the class there as the first field trip of the year. This event can be a great community-building activity. The discussions that lead up to a field trip (how to follow school rules when you're off school grounds, how to work together to take notes with partners, and so on) all provide great opportunities to work together and learn from one another.

For this first field trip, keeping things simple is the key. Don't go anywhere that involves a bus. Instead, choose a place that's within easy walking distance of the school. To learn more about classroom games, special projects, and field trips, see Chapter 4 of this book, starting on page 73.

Sharing

Another component of *Responsive Classroom* Morning Meetings that really helps build community in fifth grade is the practice of daily sharing. During this sharing time, students briefly tell a piece of news from their lives or talk about how their schoolwork is going. This brief sharing helps students get to know each other better and allows everyone to feel accepted and valued. Even if you don't run a full morning meeting, set aside some time each day to have students share. Here are some points to keep in mind:

Keeping Sharing Safe for Everyone

- Check in briefly with sharers, especially on days when only a few students share. If a topic is inappropriate, review what the class discussed about rules for sharing and help the child find another topic.

- Encourage students to check in with you if they're not sure of their topic.

- Explain the goals of sharing to families. Let them know that if they have any unsettling news, they should talk about it with you or remind their child to share it only with you.

- React calmly if a student does share something inappropriate. Gently end the sharing, trying not to embarrass the student, and move on. For example: "John, that sounds like something you and I should talk about in private. After we talk, you can share tomorrow."

■ **Make sharing purposeful.** One of the most common fifth grade questions is "Why?" Fifth graders are usually not content to comply just because an authority figure is leading them. So be sure to let them know why sharing is important: "Sharing is a great way for us to get to know each other. The better we know each other, the better we'll be able to work together!" Also, keep sharing meaningful and relevant to their daily lives. For example, point out to students the connections between sharing and writing. If students are writing personal experience narratives or poetry, they might use the stories that are shared during morning meeting as inspirations for writing later in the day.

■ **Keep topics appropriate.** Fifth graders can share stories about their weekend and the typical goings-on of everyday life (that is, "talk and tell"). But their sharing shouldn't include toys, stuffed animals, and the like because these kinds of sharing can become "bring and brags," which aren't conducive for building community. Also, we need to be aware that because many fifth graders straddle childhood and adolescence, they may be seeing R-rated movies or playing mature video games. It's our job to help them recognize that such things are not appropriate topics for school sharing.

The table below offers some appropriate topics and themes for fifth grade sharing.

Good Fifth Grade Sharing Topics and Themes

■ Family trips	■ Collections	**Note:** Another great way to build community early in the year is to have students brainstorm additional appropriate topics.
■ Family celebrations	■ Favorite books and authors	
■ Friends	■ Writing pieces	
■ Weekend events	■ Progress on science or social studies projects	
■ Pets	■ Possible career interests	
■ Sports events	■ Special talent or skill	
■ Favorite music and movies		

■ **Keep sharing brief.** Use interactive modeling to teach students how to share the main idea and a few supporting details of a story. Then teach everyone how to ask skillful questions and make connections to help the whole class explore a story in a little more depth. A crisp pace to sharing keeps students focused, so encourage students to talk with each other at another time if they want to continue the discussion.

Learn More about Sharing at www.responsiveclassroom.org

Search on "sharing" and check out *The Morning Meeting Book* by Roxann Kriete (Northeast Foundation for Children, 2002).

■ **Mix up sharing formats.** Some days, plan for just one, two, or three students to share while the rest of the class listens and responds. Other days, invite students to chat with partners or in small groups. Or have them simply take turns around the circle, each student sharing weekend plans or the name of a favorite book. Remember to keep in mind the importance of modeling and practicing each format as it's introduced. See Chapter 2, "Schedules and Routines," pages 37–41, for more on interactive modeling.

63

Class Celebrations

Another wonderful way to build community with fifth graders is to have a celebration together. For fifth graders, class celebrations can serve as a great culminating event to a big curricular unit or as a fun way to relax at the end of a productive week of learning.

Purposeful Celebrations

Whatever the occasion, keep celebrations meaningful and connected to the content of the classroom. For example, as a culminating event to a unit on westward expansion, students might set up re-creations of the Lewis and Clark expedition. You could invite other classes, staff, and parents in for a "tour" of the expedition. Or, if you've just finished a big math unit on geometry, ask students to create a two- or three-dimensional design that incorporates what they've learned. Then, share these designs at an all-school assembly.

A class celebration can also be as simple as letting students have a special healthy snack while reading their poetry together. The message in all of these celebrations is clear: We care about learning. We're proud of our accomplishments. Use these special events to bring your classroom community to a new level!

What about Holidays?

Celebrating holidays can be tricky in schools. We don't want to ignore important cultural events in our society, yet we don't want to alienate students who may not celebrate these holidays. We also don't have lots of extra time to spend on events not directly related to our curriculum, and a big holiday party can disrupt an entire day (or more) of learning. The key here is to craft celebrations that honor the special time of year, are inclusive of all students, and support the academic curriculum. The following table offers a few possible alternatives to traditional holiday celebrations.

Alternatives to Traditional Celebrations

Occasion	Activity	Curricular Connections
Halloween	**Wax museum.** Make sure students understand what a wax museum is. Then have them design costumes and props that represent one of their favorite fictional characters. Set up a wax museum in the classroom with students dressed up and posed as their characters. Then invite other classes and parents to walk through and visit with the characters.	**Reading.** Invite students to choose a character from a book they've read recently. The wax museum could also be a great culmination to an author or genre study. **Writing.** Have students write a character bio to accompany their wax figure.
Christmas, Hanukkah, Kwanzaa, and other winter holidays	**Traditions from around the world.** Most cultures have some kind of celebration that coincides with the winter solstice. Students, individually or in small groups, could study one of these cultural celebrations and give a short research presentation to the class.	**Math.** With the help of adult volunteers, ask each group to follow a recipe for a traditional dish or snack from the culture they studied. **Science and social studies.** If you don't study world cultures in fifth grade, consider an alternative event focused on immigration and the cultures represented in your community.
Valentine's Day	**Class game day.** Instead of candy and cards, strengthen the bonds of friendship with an afternoon of playing games. You could play some whole-class games for awhile and then switch to board and card games in small groups. Add in some fun, healthy snacks and you've got a great day!	**Math.** During one of the day's game periods, use games from your math program. **Word study.** Play Boggle, Scrabble, and other word games and puzzles during another game period. **Science and social studies.** Invite students to create and play their own games based on the science and social studies units they're studying.

See Chapter 4, "Classroom Games, Special Projects, and Field Trips," starting on page 73, for more on games and special projects like these.

Recess and Lunchtime

When I first began teaching, I thought that the midday break for recess and lunch was a time when I didn't have to focus so much attention on rules and expectations. "Kids can just run around and play and hang out with friends," I thought. And for some students, I was right. These students were able to smoothly play with their friends at recess and find a table at lunch while happily chatting away with classmates.

However, this certainly wasn't true for every student. I noticed that several students wandered around at recess, not joining in games or talking with others. A few others disrupted games by running through them or chased students who didn't want to be chased. At lunch, some students ate by themselves most days while a few others acted inappropriately and bothered those around them.

I also remember being frustrated when students would come back from lunch without having eaten anything, asking if they could now eat their sandwich during our read-aloud time. At times, some students would enter the classroom glaring at others, whisper angrily to close friends, and be unable to focus on their math work. What's going on, I wondered?

As it turns out, the recess and lunch break can be the most complicated time of the day for students. Kids from multiple classes converge on the playground, often with little guidance or structure. Some kids have playground balls and some don't. Some classes get out early and others join later, after games and activities have already started. At lunchtime, students must sort themselves out at tables and may jockey for position with friends or vie for the most desirable seats. It's not exactly a recipe for a safe and relaxing midday break.

If we want students to recharge their batteries for an afternoon of learning, we need to ensure that their recess and lunch breaks are physically and emotionally safe, predictable, and fun. We may not have recess or lunch duty every day, so we won't always be there to help guide students through these periods. Yet, there's a lot we can do as the classroom teacher to prepare them for a successful recess and lunch, whether we're with them or not. After all, we want to build a stronger sense of community throughout the day, every day. Here are some ideas:

■ **Use interactive modeling.** What skills do students need to be taught so they can have a good recess and lunch break? Do students know how to ask to join a game? What should it look and sound like as students reenter the building? Do they know how to fill out lunch tickets? Do all students know how the lunch line works? Be sure to teach, model, and let students practice these and other essential skills so that they can be successful with the rules and routines of recess and lunch. See Chapter 2, "Schedules and Routines," pages 37–44, for more on interactive modeling and which routines to teach and model for recess and lunch.

■ **Work toward adult consistency.** Is jumping off the swings okay? What about running up the slide? If students want to join a game that's in progress, how should they ask? And how should others respond? Can students get up from their lunch table to get something they forgot? Is seat-saving allowed? What happens if someone leaves their lunch box in the classroom or forgets their lunch ticket? When the adults on duty answer such questions with consistency, we help create a safe, predictable—and truly enjoyable—recess and lunch. Look for opportunities to talk with colleagues about this time of day (for example, at staff meetings). If support staff help manage this time of day, work with them to set up clear and consistent rules and expectations.

■ **Provide structures for recess.** Students who often struggle to find something positive to do at recess can benefit greatly from adult-structured play that enables everyone to be included and feel safe. Early in the year, you may want to review the rules for common playground games, such as tag, freeze tag, and kickball. If you're on recess duty, play a tag game (with well-defined rules) while another adult monitors the play structure area (or vice versa). Also, ask the physical education teacher to teach recess games and provide equipment in a certain area. As the year progresses, introduce variations on these games or introduce new games, depending on children's social and physical needs.

■ **Provide structures for lunch.** For example, post question cards at tables to spark student conversation: "If you could travel anywhere, where would you go and why?" "If you could meet any famous person, whom  would you meet and what would you ask her or him?" At the beginning of the year, I assign seats in the cafeteria so that all students know where to sit, eliminating the jockeying for seats that often causes hurt feelings. As the year goes on, you might provide fewer structures if students don't seem to need them. You might also invite students to come up with ways to structure lunch so that everyone is included and safe.

■ **Be alert for struggling students.** Be aware of any students who are having a hard time engaging positively with others, such as when working as part of a group. They're often the ones who struggle the most at recess and lunch. Give these students some structured options in advance (for example, a choice to play an adult-led game or on the structure with a partner; a choice to eat with an adult in the classroom or with a lunch buddy) and then support them on the playground and in the cafeteria as needed.

■ **Play and eat with students.** Sometimes when we serve as recess and lunch monitors, we end up being either too strict or too lenient. We don't want to bark orders and get into power struggles. But we also shouldn't ignore any problem behaviors, intentional or not. When serving as a monitor, one effective approach is to get right in there and fully engage with students while they play and eat. On the play-

68

Learn More about Building Community at www.responsiveclassroom.org

The following resources provide valuable information and tips, including advice for recess and lunch.

The First Six Weeks of School by Paula Denton and Roxann Kriete (Northeast Foundation for Children, 2000).

In Our School by Karen L. Casto, EdD, and Jennifer R. Audley (Northeast Foundation for Children, 2008).

36 Games Kids Love to Play by Adrian Harrison (Northeast Foundation for Children, 2002).

"The Middle of the Day" by Gail Healy, *Responsive Classroom Newsletter*, February 2001.

Other Resources
The Ultimate Playground & Recess Game Book by Guy Bailey (Educators Press, 2000).

Elementary Teacher's Handbook of Indoor and Outdoor Games by Art Kamiya (Parker, 1985).

ground, join in a tag game or pitch in the kickball game (thus eliminating one common power struggle). At lunch, join a table that has some extra energy or one that feels too subdued.

■ **Review rules and expectations from time to time.** Recess and lunch may go smoothly for a stretch of time and then a holiday, a vacation, or some other big event approaches, and behaviors may slip a bit. Use these teachable moments to rebuild and strengthen community. Use interactive modeling to reteach any routines and expected behaviors that may have slipped.

By engaging in these ways, you can build positive relationships with students, model fair play and friendly interactions, and become a more consistent presence on the playground and in the cafeteria.

Maintaining a Strong and Positive Community

We've talked a lot about how important it is to focus on building a positive learning community at the beginning of the school year. It's also very important to work at maintaining that sense of community throughout the year. Otherwise, the class's ability to work well as a team, and their positive feelings and energy, may slip away. You can keep up the team spirit and "can-do" attitude through daily morning meetings, periodic celebrations, fun energizers, and so on. By regularly providing opportunities like these for students, you can help keep them feeling connected and ready to learn.

Also, there are key times during the school year when you'll want to focus more attention on the classroom community. For example:

■ **Returning from school vacations.** After a week (or two) away from school,

---

What's an Energizer?

Energizers are quick, whole-group activities that you can do anywhere, anytime. They can be enlivening or calming. They don't take long—three minutes or less—but they can have a big impact on learning and community building. For example, a quick game or choral reading of a poem may help ease the transition from one lesson to the next.

To learn more, check out *Energizers! 88 Quick Movement Activities That Refresh and Refocus* by Susan Lattanzi Roser (Northeast Foundation for Children, 2009), available at WWW.RESPONSIVECLASSROOM.ORG.

most students need help readjusting to the culture and climate of the classroom. Some may have had lots of unstructured time; others may be tired from a long trip; many may simply be struggling to readjust to the daily school routine. Use morning meetings and regular class discussions and reminders to refocus students on class rules and routines and on the importance of working together. If needed, use interactive modeling to reteach classroom routines.

■ **Late winter.** I'm not sure what it is about February in fifth grade, but I always notice changes in the class. Some students suddenly look about three inches taller. New fads—music, computer games, clothing, hairstyles—often appear. Friendship groups may be shifting, especially if there's a transition to new sports' schedules or afterschool activities. This is a great time to reemphasize community. Plan time for team-building activities and purposeful, small-group work in academic areas.

■ **Spring.** Change certainly is in the air! Some students experience a growth spurt late in fifth grade. Deodorant may become a pressing need. Girlfriend, boyfriend, and friendship issues may arise with greater prominence. If fifth grade is the last year at the school, middle school jitters start to intensify. All of these changes can cause anxiety

Some Tips for Dealing With Change:

■ **Worries about middle school.** Hold afternoon class meetings once a week to talk about the transition to middle school. Invite a middle school teacher or counselor (and students) to talk to the class.

■ **Social concerns.** Offer to host lunch groups in the classroom so students can talk about certain topics, such as friendship issues.

■ **Changing bodies.** If the school curriculum doesn't include formal instruction to help students understand their changing bodies, talk with a school counselor and nurse about how best to address those issues.

and affect the positive community you've all worked so hard to build over the course of the year. Time spent helping students sort out these changes in safe and appropriate ways is time well spent. If we don't make this effort, these issues will inevitably disrupt academic learning and lead to hurt feelings.

■ **End of the year.** Many schools, especially K–5 schools, do a grand culminating project at the end of fifth grade. For example, some schools have all their fifth graders go on a field trip to an environmental center. School plays and science fairs are other common culminating events. Though budget cuts and standardized testing time crunches have forced many schools to cut back on these rich learning experiences, you can still organize an end-of-year project for your class of fifth graders. A multifaceted project that has students creating and presenting important work or sharing a significant experience together can help keep them energized and focused during the last months of school. For more ideas about special projects and field trips, see Chapter 4.

Closing Thoughts

It's a late fall day when I visit Carmela Barth's fifth grade classroom. Carmela invites the students, all of whom have been solving math problems, to share one problem they're proud to have solved. A trio of girls working together ask, "Mrs. Barth, is it okay if we all share the same problem?" "You're all proud of the same problem?" "Yes." "And you're each prepared to explain it?" "Yes." "Okay then." "Thanks, Mrs. Barth!" the girls say excitedly.

These fifth grade girls might seem more interested in being part of the group than in the math. But Carmela knows that having a heightened interest in relationships is a common characteristic of fifth graders. She also knows that by nurturing positive relationships and a sense of belonging, teachers can leverage these common characteristics of fifth graders to help them achieve academic goals—and feel like vital members of the classroom. When teachers do this, fifth graders feel valued, accepted, and safe, and they can more fully participate as proud members of a community of learners.

CHAPTER 4

Classroom Games, Special Projects, and Field Trips

I once had a fifth grade class that did incredible work on an ecosystems project. There were four different groups, each studying a different ecosystem. Each group was responsible for researching and presenting information in several major categories (such as flora and fauna, geography, climate, and people's impact on the ecosystem).

As part of their project, each group had to transform an area of the classroom into the ecosystem they were studying. They had to create a huge food web of the ecosystem. They had to put together a group presentation that was between twenty and thirty minutes long. And each group member had to research at least two animals of their choice from the ecosystem all on their own. This was a massive project that took us over six weeks to complete.

Fifth graders thrive when challenged appropriately with projects such as this one. They also benefit from games and field trips that focus on active and interactive learning. In fact, fifth graders will have a hard time feeling a sense of accomplishment and pride if their work is too easy or dull.

This is why I love teaching fifth grade so much. Fifth graders have great energy and passion for school when they're actively engaged in interesting work. Whether they're playing a simple game that reinforces a math concept or taking on an ambitious science project, fifth graders become fully engaged and engrossed in their work—when it's challenging and fun.

I know, I know. We've got curriculum manuals. We've got pacing guides. We've got test scores to think about. We also have classrooms full of students who look to us to make learning stimulating. It doesn't have to be either-or. With some thoughtful planning, we can cover the curriculum and help students achieve academically while making their schoolwork lively. In fact, if we make their schoolwork lively, fifth graders will learn more, astounding us with their social and academic growth.

Classroom Games

Teachers sometimes find it difficult to imagine game-playing as part of the daily curricula in fifth grade. It can seem easier to limit classroom games to downtimes or before or after learning tasks. But all kinds of amazing things happen when we incorporate engaging activities into our daily curriculum lessons as well. Students get a boost of energy. They learn more. They enjoy school. They take more positive academic risks. Lively learning can't be optional or something we do only when the classroom work is done. Instead, we need to embed games, songs, and hands-on experiential learning throughout the day.

Take some time to think about where in the day you can replace some of the less-active learning tasks. For example, instead of having fifth graders practice multiplication facts while sitting still, have the class skip-count aloud, sitting and standing at each multiple: 7 (stand), 14 (sit), 21 (stand), 28 (sit), and so on. You could also embed active tasks during a read-aloud time. When reviewing what's happened in the book so far, you could form small groups of students and assign each a scene from the book to act out. Each group practices for a few minutes and then performs a skit.

A lesson could start or end with a short game that reinforces the academic goals the class is working toward: a quick math game before or after a geometry lesson, a brief literacy game before or after writing workshop, and so forth. Or provide opportunities for students to practice math and science skills by using manipulatives. Another idea is to ask students to create riddles, songs, and raps about topics they're currently studying. There are so many possibilities.

Students will be more engaged, have more positive energy, and achieve greater successes when learning activities are lively and active. Here are some more tips to keep in mind when playing games with fifth graders:

Good Games for Fifth Grade

■ **Group charades.** Divide the class into small groups (3–5 students per group). Assign each group something they have to make with their bodies or act out together—silently and with no props. For example, students could act out vocabulary words or, if they're studying geometry, form different shapes. Their classmates try to guess what they're acting out. (This activity requires a degree of risk-taking that makes it appropriate for the middle of the year or later, when the classroom community tends to be fairly strong.)

■ **Dice and card games.** You can use many variations of simple card and dice games for math practice. For example, a small group of students take turns rolling the dice to create a fraction (a three and a six can either be $\frac{3}{6}$ or $\frac{6}{3}$). Each turn, students add their fractions together. The goal is to get to exactly 10.

Another simple game is to have student partners practice long multiplication using playing cards. They draw a few cards (as many as fits the challenge level they need) and use the numbers drawn to create a multiplication problem to solve. For example, a hand of 3, 6, 9, 8, and 2 could turn into 98 x 362 or 8 x 2639.

■ **My Bonny Lies Over the Ocean.** Do you know this simple song? It serves as a great energizer when your class needs a bit of movement. The class sings the song. Every time they sing the letter *b* ("My Bonny lies over . . ."), they stand if they're sitting or sit if they're standing. The song can be sung at a variety of speeds. It's quick, it gets the blood pumping, and it's fun!

Keep Games Light and Relaxed

Many fifth graders love competition. However, games that involve lots of pressure to win or to perform in front of a group can become exercises in anxiety and frustration. Remember how important peers are to fifth graders. Think of how embarrassing it would be to forget a math fact or the capital of the state you live in if you were up in front of a whole class.

So keep games low-key and relaxed. Limit games where there's a final score (and therefore winners and losers). Also avoid games that require students to recall facts or think quickly in front of the group unless students can choose to give answers when they know them or volunteer to be asked questions.

Have the Whole Class Compete as a Group

Though competitive games can result in anxiety and even humiliation, sometimes competition can add an element of excitement and challenge. For instance, you might run a whole-class scavenger hunt in which students find as many different examples of parallel lines as they can throughout the room. Set a class goal with a time limit and see how students do when acting as one team. This kind of competition can help promote a learning community, rather than break it apart.

Keep Games Relevant

Make sure that the games you introduce have a clear learning purpose that reinforces what the class is studying—and explain that purpose to students. For example, if the class is studying fractions, students could play a game with dice that helps them practice comparing and ordering fractions. Or they could play a game with money to help them with decimals. Name the practice students are getting as the reason they're playing these games.

Learn More about Games for Fifth Graders at www.responsiveclassroom.org

99 Activities and Greetings: Great for Morning Meeting . . . and other meetings, too! by Melissa Correa-Connolly (Northeast Foundation for Children, 2004).

Energizers! 88 Quick Movement Activities That Refresh and Refocus by Susan Lattanzi Roser (Northeast Foundation for Children, 2009).

Doing Math in Morning Meeting by Andy Dousis and Margaret Berry Wilson (Northeast Foundation for Children, 2010).

Play Throughout the Day

There have been times when I've caught myself saying to students, "You can play a game if you finish your real work," or "We'll do a movement activity if we have time at the end of the period." This is a mistake. If we don't provide chances for students to move and be playful all day long, they'll figure out ways to meet these needs on their own. They'll fidget. They'll crack jokes at the wrong time. They'll doodle instead of listening to the math lesson. Instead of offering fun and movement as a reward, make movement and fun the norm! If, for example, you notice students' energy level dropping in the mid-afternoon, opt for a quick energizer to get everyone moving.

Teach the Necessary Skills

Use interactive modeling to teach students any skills they'll need for successful game playing, such as how to toss an object gently and how to move their bodies in a small space without hitting others. Also teach students how to make the transition from an energizer to their next academic task. See Chapter 2, "Schedules and Routines," pages 37–41, for a full explanation of interactive modeling.

Special Projects

Fifth graders are primed for great project work. As a general rule, they can read well enough to successfully access a variety of texts, such as fiction, textbooks, and websites. They tend to have good fine-motor control, which makes cutting, coloring, gluing, constructing, painting, molding, and other artistic tasks doable and fun. For the most part, they're prepared (and very excited) to use technology to produce meaningful work through blogs, wikis, webpages, online presentations, and more.

Rapidly developing social skills also make fifth grade a prime year for projects. Students can mentor younger children, work collaboratively with partners and in small groups, interview adults, and work on various projects in a myriad of ways.

Whether you're considering a small project, such as creating dioramas to share books that students have read, or a much larger project, such as making a class documentary about the Industrial Revolution, keep the following guidelines in mind.

Make Sure Projects Are Meaningful to Students

Did you ever have to produce formulaic book reports? Have you ever had to write a paper or do a project that only the teacher would see? Have you ever had an assignment where you've thought, "Why am I doing this?" Fifth graders are asking that question more and more. In fact, I like to encourage students to ask that question.

Projects should have a purpose that students care about. They might write letters to an author because they want to connect with someone whose writing has influenced them. They can create posters about environmental issues to prompt people to change—to use less water or to recycle more. They might put on a play or create a movie to share their vision with an audience. As you plan projects, big and small, always ask this question: If I were a student about to take on this project, why would I care about it? Why is it relevant to me and what I'm studying?

Offer Students Choices

When you can, give students options, within broad guidelines, for what they learn or how they learn it. Having a say in the learning goals helps students become more invested in their work. There are lots of ways to give students options when they're doing project work. For example, students could choose the books they read for a biography study. Or the whole class might read the same biography, but then students create a project of their choice about the person's life. If the project is to create a bulletin board to showcase the class's work on fractions, students could choose to design their own posters, charts, or other two-dimensional displays of fractions. This kind of student empowerment helps students see the work in the classroom as their work, not as work for the teacher.

Plan Student Groups Carefully

Students in fifth grade usually love to work with a partner or in a small group. There are times, however, when it makes more sense for them to work on their own. Occasionally, you might even give students a choice about whether to work on their own or with others.

When deciding how to group students for project work, consider the goals of the project. If the goal is for students to demonstrate knowledge gained or to share personal thoughts, individual projects might be best. Perhaps the goal is for students to do complex investigations into a challenging issue (for example, to explore responsible stewardship of the environment). If so, then small groups might work best because of the scope of the project and the need for collaboration.

Learn More about Academic Choice
at www.responsiveclassroom.org

Learning Through Academic Choice by Paula Denton, EdD (Northeast Foundation for Children, 2005).

Here are some suggestions for designing effective group work:

■ **Keep groups small.** Two or three students are usually better able to remain on task and be productive than groups of four or five. If larger groups are required, consider breaking them into subgroups, and give each subgroup a specific task to do.

■ **Choose the groups.** In general, it's best if you assign students to groups, especially for long-term or complex projects. This way, you can match students' temperaments, skills, and other attributes to form effective teams. If you're okay with random groupings of students, I suggest pulling names out of a hat. Avoid letting students pick their own partners or groups. Invariably, the student choice method results in some students feeling excluded—whether or not they were intentionally excluded—and will hurt your efforts to build a positive learning community.

■ **Structure roles.** Clarify what each student in the group should be doing. At the beginning of the work period, you could provide a list of tasks and have group members discuss who will take on each. Or you might assign specific roles in the group. Either way, be sure that students understand their individual responsibilities so that everyone can be productive and successful.

Plan Projects That Include Active Learning

For example, students who are studying statistics and graphing in math could each design their own survey to conduct in another classroom or area of the school. After they administer their surveys, they could create graphs and share their results.

In one fifth grade I visited, the students were studying rocks and minerals. But instead of just reading information out of their textbook and answering questions, they scoured the playground for rocks and then worked in small teams to classify the rocks according to the information in their textbooks. It wasn't nearly as easy as they had thought it would be, and they had many lively discussions about which rocks belonged to which categories. In the end, the students didn't all agree on the categorizations, but they had all been doing work that was much more like real science. They were active and engaged in their learning.

Use Constructive Assessments

After a colleague visits your classroom to observe a lesson, what do you want to hear? As for me, I want to know what she liked and what she learned. I want to know the positive things that she saw. I also want to know what suggestions she has for how I could improve my lesson next time around. These are the same kinds of assessments that we can use to help students.

Here are some ideas for constructive student assessments:

- **Assess work in progress.** All too often in schools, we wait until projects are finished before assessing them. By this time, the work is usually done and it's hard for students to make use of anything they learn from the assessment. Instead, provide assessments throughout the project so students can hear what they're doing well and learn how to make improvements before they finish.

- **Be specific.** Tell students what they've done well and what could be better, focusing on the specific attributes of their work. Here's an example of feedback that I might offer about a food web a student is working on for

Great Projects for Fifth Grade

There are many engaging projects for fifth graders to tackle, covering content-area goals as well as interdisciplinary goals. Here are just a few ideas to consider (or to use as a springboard in designing your own projects):

■ **The great egg drop.** Fifth grade teacher Mike Guarraia challenges students to create a shoebox "space capsule." The goal is to make it so well-cushioned that it could protect a raw egg from impact upon "reentry" to Earth. Students use packing peanuts, tape, paper, foam . . . anything they think can work. On the big day, the whole school gathers outside the building and watches Mike heave the shoeboxes into the air from the roof. After they land, students scramble to see whose egg survived and explore the reasons why it did or did not.

■ **Class movie.** Creating a movie together can be a lot of fun for students, and it's much more manageable than it was ten years ago, thanks to video-editing software. One year, my students retold the story of the Lewis and Clark expedition by writing a screenplay and producing a movie about it. They researched historical details, created costumes, revised and edited the screenplay, drew murals for backdrops, and memorized their lines. I've also seen fifth graders create and record short skits on science topics.

Video-editing programs allow students to easily cut and paste scenes together as well as add sound and visual effects. If you're not comfortable guiding students through these tasks yourself, enlist the help of a technology coordinator at school or a tech-savvy parent.

■ **Multigenre autobiographies.** Jen Dunham, another fifth grade teacher, has students create autobiographies using a rich variety of media. Some students perform songs, some paint pictures, and others create a sculpture of themselves. All use writing in some form as part of their autobiographies: song lyrics, poetry, essays, and so on.

■ **Independent learning projects.** Students choose a topic they're interested in exploring, with the teacher providing the structure to meet academic goals. For example, if the goal is for students to demonstrate their grasp of five nonfiction elements they've been studying, students could create a story on a topic of their choice that incorporates those elements.

81

More Great Projects for Fifth Grade

Short Projects (1–3 class periods)	Medium Projects (3–5 class periods)	Complex Projects (2+ weeks)
■ Create a diorama.	■ Design and carry out a science experiment.	■ Write a daily blog.
■ Design a poster.	■ Create a board game.	■ Set up and run a class store.
■ Create a puppet.	■ Design a webpage.	■ Write and perform a class play.
■ Design a cereal box.	■ Create a mural.	■ Design a reenactment of a historical event.
■ Write and perform a short skit.	■ Plan and carry out a short community service project.	■ Plant and maintain a class garden.
■ Conduct an interview.	■ Build a model.	■ Start and maintain a recycling program.
■ Reenact a scene or explain a concept through mime.		■ Investigate a complex topic through group research.
■ Share information by writing new lyrics to a well-known song.		

an ecosystems project: "This food web has lots of information. You've got thirty-five different plants and animals represented, which shows just how complex a food web can be in the Arctic. You've also shown how many different animals rely on small rodents as a food source. It's a bit hard to see some connections in places. In your second draft, using colored pencils or thin markers might help you show all the connections in a clearer way."

■ **De-emphasize grading.** Grading often ends discussion. I once typed out one-page narrative assessments for each fifth grader in the class as a final reflection on their independent research projects. At their request—"We're gonna be in middle school soon, Mr. A. We need to get used to grades!"— I also added a letter grade at the bottom of each paper. The students all did the same thing: They saw the grade and didn't read the narrative! If you have to use letter grades, keep them as low-key as possible.

Keep Projects Challenging and Manageable

Fifth graders thrive if they're appropriately challenged. If the work is too easy, they won't feel truly inspired by it or proud of what they've done. At the same time, fifth graders can still get overwhelmed by complex projects without sufficient guidance and support from us.

When fifth graders engage in rigorous and extended project work, we need to help them divide large tasks into smaller ones. For example, I work with students to create checklists, both for their group as a whole and for themselves individually, helping them to break the work into bite-sized chunks. To help them organize their papers, I also give each group member a folder to use for personal notes and information, and I give each group a group folder for whole-group work.

Before each work period, I have groups discuss their goals so that they know what they're trying to accomplish that day. Dividing larger tasks into smaller chunks enables fifth graders to stay focused—and energized—throughout a complex, long-term project.

Learn More about Children's Research Projects at www.responsiveclassroom.org

The Research-Ready Classroom: Differentiating Instruction Across Content Areas by Mike Anderson and Andy Dousis (Heinemann, 2006).

Learning Through Academic Choice by Paula Denton, EdD (Northeast Foundation for Children, 2005).

83

Field Trips

I remember well the day before a field trip to walk the Freedom Trail in Boston and visit important historical sites. We spent the last part of that school day getting ready for the trip, collecting notebooks, pens, and other supplies. We also reviewed our research questions, double-checked group assignments, and went over the schedule one last time. Students were getting more and more excited while I was getting more and more stressed!

That night, I lay in bed tossing and turning, running over all the details in my mind: *Jeremiah still hasn't brought in his permission slip . . . what if he forgets tomorrow? Do I have the first-aid kit ready to go? What if . . . Ugh! This is so stressful! Why do I put myself through this?*

Why indeed? Once we got there, that question was answered loud and clear. Students excitedly explored the Granary Burying Ground: "Look! Here's the grave of Crispus Attucks! He was killed at the Boston Massacre!" "Whoa, Mr. A! I just learned that people used to try to rob graves!" "Hey, Liza! Here's John Hancock's grave! Aren't you studying him?" Next we moved on to Faneuil Hall and then to Old South Meeting House, where students reenacted the debate that led up to the Boston Tea Party. Walking through Paul Revere's house was a great way to end our journey: "Look how small the beds are! You mean three kids would all sleep in that one bed?" "Can you imagine trying to cook dinner in the fireplace?"

Field trips can be unbelievably enriching and exciting learning experiences for fifth graders. They're primed to take advantage of field trips in ways that they couldn't have been in the earlier grades. They can jot quick notes as they walk and listen to speakers. They have the stamina to keep going for a full day of walking, talking, and learning. They're curious and want to put their powers of observation to the test; they're eager to find and collect information and ideas as they travel.

So how do we plan and structure field trips that are productive and fun for fifth graders and manageable for teachers and parents? Here are some tips:

Where Should the Class Go?

Simple trips can be as productive as elaborate ones, so field trips don't have to be as complicated as a visit to a major historic site. In fact, many of the field trips that I took classes on were much simpler than the Boston trip I described above.

■ **Keep trips relevant to the curriculum.** Every field trip should be connected to the curriculum and help strengthen students' learning. For example, a short nature walk in a nearby park or neighborhood could be tied to a unit on rocks and minerals or on biodiversity.

■ **Look for local spots.** What sites and resources are close by the school? Are there local historical landmarks within walking distance? Is there a conservation area or nature preserve within a short school bus ride? Does a student's family have connections to sites that tie in to the curriculum?

A trip to a store or restaurant can be a great way to make connections to the math skills students are learning in school or help them explore economics and the world of work.

■ **Keep it affordable.** Although a trip to the aquarium might be a great way to research ecosystems, it may be out of reach financially for many families if they're expected to pay for tickets and special exhibitions. Asking families to tell you if they need financial help can be embarrassing, so avoid this common practice. Instead, find ways to keep costs low so that all children can participate with pride. You could hold a fundraiser or apply for a PTO grant if a trip will cost more than a few dollars. Ask local companies for donations or try one of the resources listed on page 20. (Be sure to follow school and district guidelines for fundraising.)

What Should the Class Do?

In fifth grade, a field trip where students walk around, look at stuff, listen to a speaker, and then go home is probably not the best use of their time. To get maximal benefit out of field trips, make sure to give students active, challenging learning tasks before, during, and after so that the trip becomes an essential part of their learning.

■ **Set goals.** What's the purpose of the trip? Are students gathering information about a topic as part of a class unit? Is it the culmination of a bigger project? What are students trying to learn, and how will they use that learning when they get back to school? Once you've clarified the goals to yourself, explain them to the class. Then have students set their own specific goals within or in addition to the broad goals for the whole class: What questions do they want to answer? What do they hope to experience? How will this trip help them in their learning?

■ **Plan concrete tasks.** Fifth graders benefit from having clear and concrete tasks to accomplish on a field trip. Otherwise, students will likely wander and lose focus. One task could be finding answers to five questions that they have about a local factory. Or they could do a scavenger hunt with a checklist of plants and animals to look for on a nature walk. Maybe each group has a digital camera and a list of twenty different photos to take for their online portfolios.

■ Have students design some learning tasks. If we do all of the planning, thinking, and work for a trip, students often feel that the tasks are tedious, and they're somewhat uninvested in getting the most out of the trip. But when students help design

the learning tasks, they're more purposeful in their work. They learn more and remember more. And when the class gets back to school, students have more energy for reflections and follow-up work. They're also better able to connect what they learned on the trip to what they're learning in class. So, for example, instead of supplying questions students should research on a field trip, lead them in brainstorming a list of possible questions and then let each student choose five to explore.

What Are the Logistics of the Trip?

Fifth graders can spend a lot of time and energy worrying about the logistics of the trip if you don't give them clear information. Plan for the following elements and share the information explicitly with students:

■ **Grouping and seating.** The first thing fifth graders will ask about a field trip is who they'll be working with and who they'll be sitting with (if taking a bus). Assign groups and seating ahead of time. You may want to base assignments on the information students are collecting so they can collaborate more easily. Or form expert groups, where students in one group focus on a specific topic and report back to the whole class upon returning to school. To help students stay calm and focused during the trip, create groups that balance temperaments. However you group students, let them know about the groups as early as possible. This helps take the pressure off, especially for students who worry about friendships and social relationships.

■ **Bathroom, food, rest, and play breaks.** Where will students go to the bathroom? When and what will they eat? When will they get some downtime to rest and play? Planning these details in advance will make the day smoother for everyone and allow students to focus on their learning tasks. (For example, contact the school cafeteria about bag lunches. And use a map of the site or contact the site for logistical information, such as where bathrooms are located.) Make sure students know who they should tell when they need to use the bathroom so you or their chaperone always knows where they are.

■ **Emergencies.** What if someone gets sick or hurt? Do you have a student who's allergic to peanuts or bee stings? Carry a first-aid kit and any medications students might need. Check with the school nurse beforehand about how to handle these and other medical issues What if someone from school needs to get in touch with you quickly? Make sure you bring phone numbers for each parent as well as school-based contact information. Also, check to see if your school follows different food rules for field trips, such as no foods containing peanuts.

Remember to contact colleagues, including specials teachers, tutors, and reading specialists, if students will be missing their regularly scheduled times with them. Also let the school cafeteria know if your class will be missing lunch.

How Will Classroom Rules Apply on Our Trip?

This is a question that I always pose to students as we plan a field trip. It's important that students view the trip as an extension of the classroom. We raise our hands to ask questions in class, so we'll do the same thing with speakers on a trip. We walk respectfully in hallways, so we'll do the same thing in a museum. Here are some more ideas about making sure that routines and behaviors remain appropriate on trips:

■ **Anticipate behavior changes.** When out of the safe and comfortable routines of school, students sometimes get silly or anxious. Knowing that this is fairly common can help us keep our own cool when we see misbehavior. Try to empathize with students—they're most likely acting in unusual ways because they're feeling out of sorts. You can help them regain self-control quickly before any misbehavior snowballs by using brief and clear reminders ("Marie, remember we are going to walk on the sidewalk") and redirections ("Jon, keep your hands to yourself"). You might also place a student in a position that will encourage success (such as at the beginning of the line) or provide some extra adult attention for some students. For example, if I have several adult chaperones, I always place the students with the most challenging behaviors in my group so that I can help them out.

■ **Anticipate trouble spots.** It shouldn't surprise anyone that students can get loud on a school bus. It also shouldn't be surprising if students start to run around if they're eating outside. So what do we do? Let's be prepared. Have students brainstorm ahead of time when they might have a harder time staying in control. Make a list and then brainstorm strategies for following the class rules during these times. When the times are approaching on the actual trip, give a reminder: "Okay everyone, we're about to head back inside. This is one of the times we listed when it might be harder to stay in control of ourselves. Remember that other classes are busy learning. How can we be respectful in the hallways as we walk back to the classroom?"

■ **Make a backup plan.** When students struggle with following rules, we want to do everything we can to set them up for success. But we also have a responsibility to prevent the behavior of one student from ruining a trip for everyone. Having a backup plan for students with behavioral challenges is one way to ensure that all goes well. Perhaps a chaperone can sit quietly with a child who's losing control. Maybe someone from school can come and pick up a student who's disrupting learning or acting in unsafe ways.

> **Productive Waiting Time**
>
> An excellent way to keep students engaged while waiting is to bring a read-aloud book that connects to the field trip. Or, before the trip, you could have students brainstorm activities they can do with a partner or small group if they have some downtime.
>
> For example, while waiting for the bus, students can play "Double This Double That" or a similar game. While some students are on a bathroom break, others can give three clues about something they've seen so far to a partner who tries to guess what it is.

■ **Use interactive modeling.** If students have not seen how we expect them to behave in the nonschool situations they'll be in during a field trip, they can be thrown for a loop. For example, do students know how to stay with their group and walk safely through a crowded museum? Before each trip, use interactive modeling to reinforce expected behaviors, teach any new routines that students will need to know, and show them what familiar routines will look like in the field trip setting. Doing so can make or break a field trip. See Chapter 2, "Schedules and Routines," pages 37–41, for a full explanation of interactive modeling.

Make Sure to Communicate with On-Site Personnel

You've already read about that great trip to the Freedom Trail in Boston. There was one part that wasn't so great. At one location, a guide addressed the students. "I'm excited to talk with you about the American Revolution. So let's start with basics. Who were the Hessians?" Most students stared blankly. "Come on! Those were the German troops King George hired to fight the colonists." He asked several more very specific questions and each time was met with blank stares. "I thought you guys were studying the American Revolution!" he exclaimed in frustration. I cringed when I saw students looking embarrassed.

I also started to get annoyed with this guide for assuming what students should know. Then it dawned on me. I never talked with anyone from the field trip sites about students' learning goals or assignments. The guide likely assumed that this was a culminating trip to wrap up a unit. For the students, though, it was part of the kick-off to a unit. The class was using this trip to gather information, formulate questions, and explore new ideas.

This was an important lesson for me. If you're going to a site where speakers will be addressing students, talk with a contact person at the site in advance. Check on the program that's being presented to make sure it matches students' goals.

It's also a good idea to discuss the format of the site's presentation. Will students get to participate and be active learners? Too many sites expect students to just sit and listen for an extended time. Offer information and even suggestions to presenters about ways to keep students fully engaged throughout their visit.

Closing Thoughts

For many years, I experienced education solely through the eyes of a teacher. Now, as the parent of elementary schoolchildren, I also get to see it through their eyes. It's a rare day when Ethan or Carly tell me about a great math lesson. They both love to read, but I don't hear much about their daily reading at school either. Honestly, I hear more about lunch and recess than anything else. But when they do get excited enough to voluntarily talk about their learning with me, it's almost always about a fun game, or an interesting

project, or an upcoming field trip. These kinds of learning experiences are what fire kids up. This kind of work is interesting, challenging, and relevant to their lives. As teachers, we need to keep working at making games, projects, and field trips more than a once-in-a-while treat. We should make them an integral part of how we help children learn and grow.

CHAPTER 5

Communicating with Parents

Communicating with parents may be one of the most important aspects of teaching. Parents have wonderful insights into their child. I consider them invaluable allies and assets—they help me to know their child better, and that in turn helps me do a better job of teaching.

I'll be the first to recognize, however, that interacting with parents can be a bit intimidating, especially for newer teachers. One thing that can make it challenging is that every parent is unique. Just as each student has unique interests, perspectives, learning styles, gifts, and challenges, so, too, does each parent. Parents may also have a wide range of feelings about school, based on their experiences as parents, as members of the community, and as former students themselves. Similarly, parents vary in how actively they participate in the life of the school.

But the fact that parents can be so different from one another also makes working with them rewarding. Parents can often pleasantly surprise us with insights and ideas that help us understand their child and family more deeply. They may offer a perspective on an issue that we never thought of before. Sure, we'll have some challenging interactions with parents, but we'll have lots of positive ones as well.

In working with parents, we should keep firmly in mind that despite their diversity, all parents have one thing in common: They want what's best for their child, and that includes the best learning and growth at school. To enable parents to collaborate with us as partners in their child's

91

About the Term "Parent"

Students come from a variety of homes with a variety of family structures. Many children are being raised by grandparents, siblings, aunts and uncles, and foster families. All of these people are to be honored for devoting their time, attention, and love to raising children. Coming up with one word that encompasses all these caregivers is challenging. For simplicity's sake, this book uses "parent" to refer to anyone who is the child's primary caregiver.

learning, we teachers need to communicate regularly with them, keeping them informed about what's happening in the classroom in general and with their child in particular. We also need to encourage parents to take part in the life of the classroom and provide opportunities for them to do so in ways that fit into their busy schedules and feel comfortable to them. Just as importantly, we should acknowledge and honor the contributions of every family.

So, how can we do all this? And how can we communicate effectively with all parents if each one is unique? How should we respond to the concerns that parents of fifth graders often have? How can we structure parent-teacher conferences so that they're positive and productive? How can we have a fruitful two-way discussion about the struggles that a child may be having?

In this chapter, you'll get answers to these and other questions. You'll also get practical tips for developing healthy and positive relationships with each fifth grade student's family. After reading the chapter, I hope you'll feel more confident about taking the initiative, empathizing with parents, and staying in regular contact with them.

Strategies for Good Communication

Effective communication with parents is key to their positive participation in their child's school life. The more parents know about what and how their children are doing in school, the more they can play an active role in supporting their children's school success. Good communication also helps you build a positive relationship with parents, which bolsters your relationships with their children as well.

If I had to choose one piece of advice to give about communicating with parents, it would be this: Reach out to parents when you have positive news to share, not just when their child is off track. When you see a student helping a classmate with an assignment or showing some other act of kindness, call or send a quick note to let his parent know. When you observe a child working hard on an academic or social skill, share the good news with her parent.

These small but important "good news" contacts convey to parents that you see their child's positive qualities and accomplishments, which can be highly reassuring. These positive contacts also help establish trust between you and parents so that if you need to talk with them sometime about a problem their child is having, that communication is likely to be easier and more productive.

Here are a few other effective communication strategies:

Start Reaching Out Early and Often

I recommend getting in touch with parents as soon as possible. You want to learn as much as you can about the child and his or her family and start to build a positive relationship. Doing so early on will help you better meet each child's needs from the get-go.

For example, if you're lucky enough to get your class list before the previous year is finished, reach out to next year's parents right away. You could simply send a friendly email or note: "I'm really excited to be a part of your child's education for the coming year! I'd love to meet you and say 'hi.' Please stop by sometime after school if you can. I'm in Room 123."

Here are some other ways to make positive connections with families from the start:

- ■ **Welcome letter.** During the summer, send home a short letter (via regular mail or email) that introduces you and lets parents know about some of the fun and exciting work their children will be doing in fifth grade. Also let parents know when families can stop by the classroom and meet you before school starts. You can also send this letter home with children on the first day of school. (See the sample letter on the next page.)

- ■ **Informal classroom visit.** A week or two before school starts or during the first week of school, hold a casual meet-and-greet one evening. Such a gathering early in the year can be a great way to chat with parents and let them see what the classroom looks like.

- ■ **Phone calls and emails.** Once the year starts, communicate frequently with parents. However, be careful not to overwhelm them with too much information. Chances are, some parents will struggle with reading and some won't have time to sift through a lot of minute details, especially if given all at once. Short, frequent, and friendly communications set a positive tone—and are more likely to be read and remembered.

Sample Letter to Parents

Dear Parents and Caregivers,

Welcome to fifth grade! I am really looking forward to our upcoming year together. First, let me introduce myself briefly. I've been teaching for fifteen years. I've been at our school since 1999. When I'm not in school, I love to spend time with my wife, Heather, and our two children, Ethan and Carly.

This year, our class will be exploring many exciting topics. We'll do a lot of scientific thinking and work as we explore geology, simple machines, and more. In social studies, we'll focus on learning about American history. In math, we'll build on the skills students learned in fourth grade and work in new areas such as coordinate geometry and more complex problem-solving. In literacy, we'll continue to have reading workshop and writing workshop, and we'll integrate our science and social studies work into these workshops.

As the year begins, we'll spend some time getting to know each other. As we begin our academic work, we'll also work together at becoming a strong learnng community. When students feel safe and comfortable in the class-room, they're better able to take on academic challenges.

In a few weeks, we'll have our annual Back to School Night. Here are two questions to think about for that evening: What are your hopes for your fifth grader this year? What academic and social goals do you have for your child? I look forward to talking with you about these.

Please contact me if you have any questions. You can email me at mr_anderson@school.org or call me at home before 8:00 PM (XXX-XXX-XXXX). I'm looking forward to meeting you—and to a great year!

If you need help communicating with families whose primary language is not English, turn to experts at school. For example, ask a language specialist or school-home coordinator for practical tips and resources. Seek out colleagues who speak the same language as students' families and ask for their advice.

Listen and Learn

It can't be overstated: Students' parents know their children best and have a lot to teach us about them. We are privileged each year to share in the growth and development of their children in the classroom, so we need to make time to listen to and learn from parents each year. Here are a few ideas about how we can do that:

■ **"Hopes and Dreams" letter or survey.** Invite parents to write you a brief letter or jot down some notes about what they hope their child will get out of fifth grade. Encourage parents to think about academic, social, and emotional goals for their child. This information will tell you a lot about what families value and in what areas children may need extra support. You could also send home a survey for parents to fill out instead of asking them to write a letter. A survey with specific questions may seem directive, but it can be easier for some parents than writing.

95

■ **Notes and phone calls.** If you have parents who might struggle with writing you a letter or filling out a survey, send home a quick note giving everyone a heads-up that you'll be calling them soon to hear their hopes and goals for their child this school year. Then, over the course of a week, call five or six parents each night. You'll be amazed at what you learn.

■ **Home visits.** Some parents have work obligations or transportation issues that make it hard for them to come to school. Other parents are uneasy about visiting school due to negative past experiences. A good way to reach these parents is to make a brief home visit for each student at the beginning of the school year. In fact, offering to come to a child's home to meet and chat can help all parents see that you care about their child and are approachable. Seeing a home environment can also help you learn more about a child. (Be sure to follow school and district guidelines for home visits.)

Learn More about Working with Families of Different Cultures at www.responsiveclassroom.org

Parents & Teachers Working Together by Carol Davis and Alice Yang (Northeast Foundation for Children, 2005).

I can't stress enough the importance of connecting with students' parents at the beginning of the school year. By doing so, you'll learn more about how to reach and teach every student. You'll also be sending a powerful message to all parents: I value you and your family. I care deeply about your child. We are partners in your child's learning.

Be Empathetic—Especially During Challenging Moments

When a parent is angry, it's natural to get defensive or even angry in response. It's our fight or flight instinct kicking in. However, it's not very productive to flare up and fight back or to run and hide in the supply closet. Instead, a simple shift in perspective can make a huge difference in how we react.

Remember that anger is usually a secondary emotion. In my experience, parents who are angry are often scared first. They're scared for their child. They may be worried that he or she isn't learning enough. Or they may be afraid that their child is being teased, bullied, or excluded. They may be reliving one of their own negative school experiences as they watch their child struggle.

So here's the shift we can make. When a parent comes to us and says, "I've got to talk to you about something! I am so mad!" we can try to shift our

---

Share Information about Child Development with Parents

The more we help parents understand child development, the better they can support their child. And knowing that we're mindful of child development issues as we plan their child's learning helps parents develop trust in us. Here are some key ideas to convey to parents:

- **Human growth and development is complex.** No two children reach a particular milestone at the same time. For example, some fifth graders will begin to enter adolescence while others will remain firmly in childhood. Some students may seem much older or younger emotionally or cognitively than their peers. This diversity of development is very common throughout fifth grade.

- **Physical, cognitive, and social growth rates may differ.** The tallest student in the class may appear emotionally young. A student who has made huge gains as a reader over the past three months may plateau for a while, consolidating recent growth. For many children, growth happens in fits and starts.

- **Children will change as the year progresses.** A student may begin the year appearing easygoing and relaxed, which is a fairly common characteristic of fifth graders. By the middle or end of the year, this same child may appear more moody, a trait commonly seen in sixth graders.

perspective and hear, "I've got to talk to you about something! I am so scared!" Consider how your emotions also shift once you change your perspective. When you hear someone tell you they're mad, you tense up and get ready to fight or flee. When you hear someone tell you they're scared, you open up and become empathetic. You're ready to listen. You move into problem-solving mode.

Parents want what's best for their child. They may struggle with how to advocate effectively for her or him, but our job is to help their child as best we can. By controlling our own emotions and listening to parents with empathy, we're more likely to work as a team and achieve our shared goals for their children.

Communicate Regularly and Consistently Throughout the Year

It's important to continually keep parents informed about what's happening in the classroom and in school. The more they know, the more they can help support their child's school life. But once the school year is well under way, it can be easy to lose touch with parents. Projects start to build, paperwork starts to pile up, and meetings multiply. Before we know it, a few weeks have gone by and we're no longer communicating regularly.

Creating a simple system for communicating with parents and building it into our weekly routine is the key to success here. When we make communication a regular habit, it's much easier to keep it going. Here are a few tips:

■ **Circle notebooks.** Give every child a school-home notebook. Each Friday, have students attach to a notebook page a brief letter from you that gives their parents some highlights from the week and reminders for upcoming events. Some teachers even include a photo with their letter. Next, students write their own letter about the week to their parents in the notebook. Parents then respond over the weekend, writing as much or as little as they want, and send the notebook back to school on Monday. (The notebook travels in a circle, from teacher to student to parent to teacher—thus, the name.)

- **Classroom webpage.** You may already have a classroom webpage through the school's website. If most families have access to the Internet, this can be a great weekly communications tool. Pick a day each week to update the class webpage, recapping the previous week's work and fun. You could write a brief note or a bulleted list of events. Pictures and video clips can also be included (check school policy before putting students' images online). As the year goes on, invite students and parents to help with the updates. They can note progress on projects or share news about a future field trip.

Find Child Development Resources for Parents at www.responsiveclassroom.org

Yardsticks: Children in the Classroom Ages 4–14 by Chip Wood (Northeast Foundation for Children, 2007), or the child development pamphlets based on this book.

Other Resources
How To Talk So Kids Will Listen & Listen So Kids Will Talk by Adele Faber and Elaine Mazlish (Harper, 1999).

- **Friday update.** Here's a simple but effective way to communicate: Each Friday, send home with students a short letter that briefly summarizes the important events of the week. For greater appeal, use colored paper, bulleted lists, and simple info-graphics. And remember to keep letters short and sweet. They'll be easier for you to write—and easier for busy parents to read.

Special Concerns of Fifth Grade Parents

Certain concerns seem to come up consistently among fifth grade parents. Knowing that these issues are likely to arise can help you address them more effectively.

Will My Child Be Ready for Middle School?

If fifth grade is the last grade in the elementary school where you teach, this question is always on parents' minds. Many parents think of middle school as a time of social turmoil and angst. It's also a time when academic expectations start to increase. So parents have legitimate concerns about the transition from elementary school to middle school. The first thing we need to do is listen to and recognize these worries. Then we need to let parents know what we're doing to help prepare their child for this next step.

■ **Communicate with the sixth grade teachers.** Ask them to describe how previous students have transitioned to the middle school. What has generally gone well? What have been the most challenging parts of the transition? What skills are most important for students to have as they enter sixth grade? You might then communicate this information directly to parents. Certainly use this information to prepare students for sixth grade and explain to parents what you're doing.

■ **Talk with parents and students who have moved on to the middle school.** Talk with parents who have had a child transition from elementary to middle school (ask at the middle school or your school for parents who may be willing to chat with you) and ask them about their child's experience. What worked well? What could have been better? You might even ask some experienced middle school parents if they would be willing to act as a resource for current fifth grade parents. Or you might compile a list of parental advice from experienced parents and pass it along to the current fifth grade parents.

■ **Know about transition meetings.** Middle schools often plan open house events or parent question-and-answer evenings for families with children who are about to move to middle school. In many elementary schools, fifth graders take a "mini" field trip to the middle school near the end of the school year. Know when these events are scheduled so you can let the fifth graders and their parents know about them in advance. Just knowing that these events are planned can help parents feel more comfortable.

■ **Communicate frequently about the challenging work that students are doing.** Sometimes I think that parents envision a sharp contrast between elementary school and middle school. They may think that work is easy and playful in elementary school and rigorous and tough in middle school. If so, they may worry that fifth grade work isn't challenging enough. Be sure to let parents know about the exciting and challenging work their fifth graders are doing. This can help reassure parents that their children are being well-prepared academically for middle school work.

- **Help alleviate student worries.** Parents will worry when their children worry. Help fifth graders get their questions and concerns about middle school answered throughout the year, but especially in the spring. Have some sixth grade students pop by one afternoon to talk about their experiences transitioning to middle school.

What about Cell Phones, the Internet, and Cyberbullying?

I was in the middle of running a math group one day when I looked over and saw one boy in tears. "Jamie? What's up?" I asked as we settled down to chat. "Jeremy, Stefan, and Ian all hacked into my online game account. They stole all my powers and made my character do really dumb moves."

Not that long ago, navigating the cyberworld was an issue that rarely came up in fifth grade. Today, more and more fifth graders are cybersavvy. They're playing online games. Some have social networking accounts. Many have cell phones and easy access to computers (often with unlimited, unsupervised Internet access).

Even if not all students are using technology so extensively, there's a good chance that cyber issues will arise in fifth grade. Schools and parents both struggle with these issues. So what can we do?

- **Know (and communicate) your school's policies about technology use.** Can students bring cell phones? If so, do the phones have to stay in backpacks and be used for emergencies only? What happens if a student brings a cell phone to recess? How do students access the Internet at school? What sites can they visit? Most schools have detailed policies about such things. Know these policies and regularly communicate with parents about them. When parents have this information, they can better support responsible technology use and bullying prevention efforts.

- **Stay current yourself.** It's hard to understand the cyberworld that students are experiencing and help them and their parents navigate it unless you also experience that world. Now, I'm not suggesting that you start playing online games. But I am suggesting that you at least become familiar with them, with social networking sites, and with other aspects of this world. For example, if you don't want to open a social network account yourself, find a friend or relative who has one and poke around the site with him or her.

■ **Have frequent class meetings about cyberbullying and tell parents about them.** Cyberbullying can happen at any school. And just because you don't hear about it doesn't mean it's not happening. Take the initiative and discuss the topic openly with students and parents. Hold class discussions about cyberbullying to help students share experiences, ask questions, and express concerns. (If students report any form of bullying at these meetings, follow school and district policies about forwarding that information to the appropriate officials.) And be sure to communicate with parents what you and the school are doing, and why, so that they can support these efforts.

■ **Help parents understand the importance of reporting cyberbullying.** It's vital that parents also understand and support the school's efforts to teach children to report incidents of mean behavior in the cyberworld (or anywhere else) to an adult. When students report such incidents, problems can be addressed promptly and students can get needed help before situations escalate.

What about Friends?

As teachers, we typically focus on lessons, units, assessments, activities, and skills. Guess what students are focused on much of the time? That's right—friends. Friendships become increasingly important in fifth grade as students start to shift from childhood to adolescence.

Parents can be confused by this shift and ask you for help figuring it out. "I don't get it! Maria and Jenny have always been such good friends. Now they seem mad at each other all the time." "Taj is really wishing he had a best friend, but he isn't into sports, and that seems to be what most of the boys in his class are interested in."

So what can we do to help? As with any parental concern, we can listen and be empathetic. We can let parents know that it's common for friendships to change as children grow up. We might also suggest that kids with similar interests get together after school or on the weekend. Or we can encourage kids to explore afterschool activities that will help them meet new friends. We can also keep an eye on social dynamics in hallways and the cafeteria and on the playground. Subtle exclusion and bullying often take place in these areas.

Finally, talk to a school counselor for more ideas about helping students and their families. Let parents know that they're always welcome to discuss issues directly with a school counselor if they prefer.

What about Changing Bodies?

I'll never forget the day that a fifth grader came up to me with tears in her eyes. "Mr. A, can I go to the nurse? I think I'm getting my first period." "Yes! To the nurse!" I declared, relieved that we had a school nurse. I also remember the first time I had "The Deodorant Talk" with fifth graders. It was a warm spring day and they had just come back from recess. It was time to talk about hygiene.

There's no doubt that fifth grade is a time of great physical changes for many children. By the middle of the year, the differences in students can be startling. Some students, especially girls, may shoot up in height and be well into puberty; other students may still look like young children. These changes can be very confusing for both students and parents.

I suggest meeting these issues head-on. Include timely reminders for parents that personal hygiene is becoming increasingly important. Remind students that they should bathe or shower regularly. Many schools integrate this teaching into their science, health, or wellness programs. If so, make sure you learn what content is being covered and know what your role will be in the program.

Homework

In many homes, homework battles are nightly occurrences. Parents often feel compelled to force children to get their work done. Some parents see homework as the mark of a rigorous school experience and expect teachers to assign plenty of it. Children, however, may feel unmotivated or overwhelmed, especially if the homework seems confusing or excessive. The following tips can help make homework go more smoothly for students and their families.

- **Set clear and reasonable guidelines.** The beginning of the year is the best time to establish and communicate manageable homework guidelines for both students and parents. For example, I suggest that students spend no more than forty-five minutes on homework on any given night, including reading for twenty minutes or so.

- **Keep homework bite-sized.** Once you establish a time frame, be sure to assign homework that fits within that expectation. Ideally, any homework will be work that students can do independently. For example, early in the year, I have students do one or two simple homework assignments to reinforce what they learned in the classroom that day or to help them prepare for the next day's lessons.

- **Teach and practice homework skills.** It's important that students develop effective homework skills, including time management strategies. These skills will help them throughout their school and work careers by giving them practical skills and boosting their confidence. For the first few weeks of school, you might even have students do their homework in class. Then gradually increase their responsibility for doing it at home.

103

Homework Help at www.responsiveclassroom.org

"Homework Blues?" *Responsive Classroom Newsletter*, November 2003.

"Homework! Strategies to overcome the struggles and help all students," *Responsive Classroom Newsletter*, November 2000.

"Is Homework Working?" *Responsive Classroom Newsletter*, January 2006.

Other Resources
Rethinking Homework: Best Practices That Support Diverse Needs by Cathy Vatterott (ASCD, 2009).

■ **Communicate with parents about their role in homework.** Inevitably, some parents will still see their children struggle with homework, no matter how well we set it up initially. Let parents and students know what to do if these struggles occur. You might have a page on the class website that has each day's homework assignment posted (guide a student in updating it each day). You could also set up a buddy system so that students can phone a friend if they forget the assignment or need some help.

In addition, I make it a point to release parents from the responsibility of getting their child to complete homework. I announce at open house night: "I'm the one assigning the homework. I'll hold students accountable for it. You are free to not force your student to do their homework. I'll take care of that issue with them in class. If I need help, I'll be sure to let you know." Ask colleagues for suggestions and use the resources listed in the "Homework Help" box on page 103 to learn more about helping students with homework—and avoid forcing them to stay in during recess to do so!

■ **Guide parents who want more homework for their child.** Consider how to help out parents who want their child to do more work—without making homework assignments too complex for you, them, or their child. For example, suggest websites that allow students to play challenging math or word games. Or suggest joining a club at school, such as a science club.

Holding Productive Parent-Teacher Conferences

When you attend a meeting, what helps you to fully participate? Likely, you appreciate knowing ahead of time what the goals and agenda for the meeting are so that you can prepare for it. You may also want to know what to bring, such as note-taking materials and other supplies. Finally, you'll want to know exactly where and when the meeting will be held.

When we host parent-teacher conferences, we're inviting parents to attend a meeting that we're facilitating. Giving them information in advance will help them prepare for our meeting and get a better sense of what to expect. Here are more ideas to help make these meetings productive and positive:

Be Thoughtful about the Setting

Sitting on opposite sides of a large desk or table creates a barrier between people and can also be intimidating. Try to set up a conference space so that you and the parent sit together at a table, where you can easily see each other and look at work samples together. Make sure that the lighting is pleasant and the room quiet. Offer adult-sized chairs so parents have an option for seating that is most comfortable for them. Be welcoming and make friendly eye contact. These important tone-setters help parents feel at ease, respected, and valued.

If parents bring their student or younger children, have books, crayons, paper, and other supplies set up so children can entertain themselves while you meet with their parents. Sometimes parents arrive early, or a preceding conference runs a little long, so have things for parents to explore while they wait, such as samples of student work and hallway displays. Also plan how to end the conference. For example, if time is running out, set up another time to talk rather than rush through the meeting.

Begin by Highlighting the Positives

Parents are often nervous when they sit down for a conference, so it's important to start with what's going well for their child. Point out specific accomplishments, skills, and qualities. For example: "Marco has really been doing well in reading lately and seems to be enjoying a wide variety of books. I've been impressed with how focused he is during reading time and how many personal connections he makes when reading."

Also, have work samples on hand to reinforce your points. For instance, if a student has read a wide variety of books during reading workshop, have his book log on hand. If a student has been doing well with a particular math concept, have a few pages of her math journal tagged and ready to share. If you want to talk about how respectful a student has been, list a few examples in advance and share them with the family. Beginning a conference with the student's strengths and positive attributes helps frame the conference as a positive one.

Tackle Only One or Two Challenges

After sharing some positives, talk about a few things that you plan to work on with the child. All children have next steps to take and challenges to work on. For some, these challenges may be front and center in your mind, and your list may be long. But be careful not to overwhelm parents with more than one or two challenges at the conference. Know that there will be time to address other issues as the year goes on. A long list may lead parents to become angry or defensive or overly harsh with their child.

In addition to keeping your list of challenges short, also be ready with ideas and suggestions for how you plan on working with the child to meet these challenges. Showing parents that you have a plan will reassure them that you're actively trying to help their child.

Finally, make sure not to spring a really big problem on a parent unexpectedly. Imagine being a parent at a conference and hearing, "Michael keeps getting into fights on the playground. He keeps punching people and picking on one student in particular!" Wouldn't you wonder why you hadn't been told this before? Even if a conference is set up to discuss a problem, parents should know the details ahead of time so that the conference can focus on possible solutions.

Invite Parents to Share Their Thoughts

Remember, parents are the experts on their children. They know them better than anyone. Effective parent-teacher conferences are just that: parent-teacher conferences. Though you, as the teacher, will be structuring and guiding the con-

How to Give Parents a Quick "FYI" about Small Incidents

Let parents know about small behavior incidents, even if they were resolved. Most small incidents don't become major problems, but if they do, these "FYI" communications will have helped prepare parents for what may need to come later, such as a problem-solving conference.

- **Call or send a note.** Since the goal is just to inform, a brief communication is usually sufficient.

- **Use a respectful, matter-of-fact tone.** Describe the incident and adult response clearly and factually. For example:

  "Victor had a bit of a challenging time at recess today. He knocked the ball out of other players' hands after someone got him out in kickball. After taking a break to calm down, he played safely and respectfully for the rest of recess and was fine the rest of the day."

You might also want to ask a colleague to review the note for clarity, tone, and appropriateness.

versation, parents should have lots of time to talk. Let parents know ahead of time that you want to hear their thoughts, opinions, and questions. Then use open-ended questions to allow parents to share ideas—for example:

❖ What do you think has been going well so far in fifth grade?

❖ What do you think are Adele's greatest strengths?

❖ What are your hopes and dreams for Ricardo this year?

Consider Inviting Students

In fifth grade, students should be taking more ownership of their learning and of their school experiences in general. I have found that having fifth graders be part of the conference can be empowering for students and enlightening for parents. For example, I've had students facilitate part of their own parent-student-teacher conferences. Students came up with a few strengths to share with their parents as well as a goal or challenge to work on. They collected work samples and evidence to explain their thinking. It was amazing how enriching these conversations were!

Learn More about Parent-Student-Teacher Conferences at www.responsiveclassroom.org

"Parent-Student-Teacher Conferences Keep the Focus on the Child" by Sadie Fischesser, *Responsive Classroom Newsletter*, April 2005.

Of course, certain conversations do need to happen just between the adults. Perhaps there's some personal information that a parent needs to share, or you may have some questions you need to ask without the student present. In these situations, students can grab a book and read in the hall or a neighboring classroom while you and the parents finish the conference.

Be Prepared to Handle Surprises

You might be surprised at what can spill out during a parent-teacher conference: "My wife and I are getting a divorce. It's just started, and the kids don't know yet." "We just got the news yesterday. I'm being relocated because of work. We're moving next week."

Sometimes problems sneak up on people, so they don't have time to tell you about them beforehand. For some parents, you may be the only person

who will listen and be empathetic. It can be hard to know what to do in situations like these. Here are some tips:

■ **If appropriate, refocus the conference.** A parent may just need to vent a little bit but may still be ready to talk about the child. If possible, help get the parent back on track: "It can be really frustrating that your ex-husband doesn't show up to conferences. If he shows up in a bit, we'll catch him up. If not, I'll give him a call later. Let's look at Dylan's reading notebook. I'm excited to show you the latest book he's been reading. . . ."

■ **Take time to think.** A parent may ask you a question that you're not sure how to answer. Or a parent may present you with information that you're unsure what to do with. Don't feel pressured to respond right away. It's okay to say, "I'd like to take some more time to think about that. I'll get in touch with you in the next few days."

■ **Go with the flow.** It's important to be well-prepared for conferences, but if something more important comes up, save what you've planned for another time. If a family is in crisis or if an important topic emerges that you hadn't planned on discussing, be prepared to change your focus. You'll likely learn valuable information.

■ **Refer the parent to a community resource,** such as a local employment center, WIC program, or support group, if he or she tells you about a struggle with unemployment or another family issue. Make sure you know and follow your school and district policies about making such referrals.

■ **If needed, get help.** If a parent becomes aggressive, abusive, or emotionally unglued, get help quickly. Depending on the situation, you might call the school office or simply walk out of the room. Or you might say, "I think we could use some help with our conference. Let's head to the office where we can talk with . . ." Again, be sure to know and follow your school and district policies for situations such as these.

Ideas for Parent Participation in Fifth Grade	
Everyday Classroom Life	**Special Events & Field Trips**
■ Photocopying, stapling, and helping with other routine tasks	■ Chaperoning field trips
■ Updating class webpages	■ Searching for websites and other resources for research projects
■ Making audio or video recordings of students reading or presenting	■ Organizing the logistics of class celebrations (making snacks, setting up, cleaning up, and so on)
■ Taking photos for digital portfolios	
■ Joining a morning meeting	■ Assisting on a big project day

Involving Parents in Events and Activities

It's pretty common for parents of younger children to regularly join classroom activities. As children get older, parents tend to participate less and less. By fifth grade, many parents seem to assume that they aren't welcome to come to school unless there's a problem or special event. However, parental involvement in fifth grade is still invaluable and essential. It can be a great way for parents to have more direct connections with their child about schoolwork.

The table above offers some ideas for ways parents can successfully participate in fifth grade.

Remember to suggest ways for parents to help even if they can't be in the classroom. For example, they could prepare something at home, such as a snack or decoration, and have their child bring it in to school. You could also ask parents to help prepare supplies for routine classroom tasks or projects, such as by tracing a pattern or cutting out geometric shapes for every student. Be sure to let the class know about the contribution of parents who may not be present for a project or special event.

For parent participation to be most effective, give parents guidelines well in advance for what to do when joining the class. (Know and follow school and district policies about inviting parents and other adults into the classroom.) So that parents can be successful and independent, they need to know what your expectations are and they need straightforward directions. Parents also need to be given tasks that they can handle well. Let's consider how we can set parents up for success.

- **Set expectations for parents.** What are the classroom rules? How do they apply to the adults in the classroom? Before parents come in to visit or participate in the classroom, send home a quick note that sets clear expectations. (See "Sample Guidelines" below.)

- **Keep groups small.** A large group of fifth graders working on an art project or walking through a zoo on a field trip together can be overwhelming for anyone. Help parent volunteers be successful by keeping their group size manageable. Three or four students is usually a good group size for times like this. Also, consider each student who will be in a volunteer's group. To address potential parental concerns of not having their child in "their" group, explain to volunteers beforehand that you will place students in groups that will allow them to be successful. Keep students who may struggle near you or another staff member so that they can get the help they need to stay in control.

Sample Guidelines for Parent Volunteers

Greetings, Parents and Caregivers! Thanks for joining us in our classroom. Here are some guidelines and information to help you out:

Class Routines

- **Hand signal/chime.** When the hand signal or chime signal is given, everyone quickly gets to a good stopping place in their conversations and work so that they're ready to listen. Adults can help by doing the same.

- **Bathroom sign-out.** Students may sign out to use the bathroom on their own. They can help explain the process if you have any questions.

Guidelines for Adults

- **Adult voices.** Adult voices can carry further than we realize and can distract learning. Please check your voice to make sure it's not too loud (I have to check this myself all the time!).

- **Discipline.** If you're working with a student or a group that is refusing to do work or is being disruptive and a simple reminder isn't enough, please let me know. I'll handle the situation quickly.

- **Privacy.** As a classroom visitor, you may see a student having a hard time. Please respect the privacy of all students by not discussing such issues outside the classroom.

If You Need to Cancel Your Visit

Sometimes you may have planned on joining us and something else will come up. That's fine. Just let me know (via email, handwritten note, or phone call) as soon as you can so I can adjust our plans.

Anything Else?

If there's anything else you're wondering about, please let me know. Thank you!

■ **Give parents nonteaching roles.** During my first years of teaching, I had parents help run reading and writing workshops. I thought this would be great, imagining all the benefits of giving students more individual attention. I even held a training session for parents one evening on running good workshops. Unfortunately, the results were less than ideal. I remember one parent took a child's writing and wrote notes all over it. Another parent kept moving over to work with his own child, even when not needed.

This was my fault. I had expected parents to pick up strategies and techniques that had taken me years to learn. On a rare occasion, you may have a parent who is also a teacher and whose philosophy matches yours. Unless that's the case, however, I recommend giving parents roles that are meaningful but that don't require direct instruction. (See the table on page 109 for ideas.)

Closing Thoughts

Before I had children of my own, I remember knowing (on some level at least) how important it was to communicate effectively with parents. And then Ethan was born. I remember coming back to school after my paternity leave and seeing students in a whole new light. They were other people's babies! Their parents had once taken them home from the hospital and spent hours just staring at their toes. Connecting with the parents of students suddenly had more meaning for me.

As Ethan and Carly get older and become more independent, I find myself relying more and more on positive school experiences to help my children grow up healthy and well-rounded. They do, after all, spend about half of every waking day at school. As teachers, we need to be mindful of the responsibility we carry, and we need to make sure that we stay in close contact with all of the parents who have entrusted their children to us. Through consistent and positive communication, we can help create effective partnerships between home and school. And when we do, we provide the support and nurturing that every student deserves.

Favorite Books, Board Games, and Websites
for Fifth Graders

Creating a classroom library, a collection of games, and a list of appropriate websites that appeal to and engage fifth graders is an important task for teachers. In this appendix, I give you a starting point for accomplishing this—suggestions for books and other resources in different categories that fifth graders enjoy and benefit from. This appendix is not intended to be a definitive list (and some items might not suit your students' interests or needs). But I hope you'll find some good ideas and resources here to help you get started.

113

Read-Aloud Books

Don't assume that fifth graders are too old for read-alouds. (Is anyone ever too old for read-alouds? As for myself, I love to listen to audio books.) Others may argue that we have too much content to teach in fifth grade to spare time for read-alouds. Au contraire! Reading aloud to fifth graders is an essential part of the day. It gives all students a shared reading experience and it offers great opportunities for class discussions and debates about academic and social content. Historical fiction is a particularly good category for read-alouds in fifth grade. Thus, I divided the list that follows into two categories.

Historical Fiction Read-Alouds

Crossing Bok Chitto: A Choctaw Tale of Friendship & Freedom by Tim Tingle

Johnny Tremain by Esther Forbes

Jordan Freeman Was My Friend by Richard White

From Miss Ida's Porch by Sandra Belton

My Brother Sam is Dead by James Lincoln Collier and Christopher Collier

CONTINUED ▶

Historical Fiction Read-Alouds continued

Like the Willow Tree: The Diary of Lydia Amelia Pierce by Lois Lowry (from the *Dear America* series by Scholastic)

Number the Stars by Lois Lowry

Out of the Dust by Karen Hesse

Pink and Say by Patricia Polacco

Sadako and the Thousand Paper Cranes by Eleanor Coerr

Shades of Gray by Carolyn Reeder

The Watsons Go to Birmingham—1963 by Christopher Paul Curtis

The Witch of Blackbird Pond by Elizabeth George Speare

Other Read-Alouds

Baseball in April and Other Stories by Gary Soto

Best Shorts: Favorite Short Stories for Sharing selected by Avi

The City of Ember by Jeanne DuPrau

The Giver by Lois Lowry

Hatchet by Gary Paulsen

Island of the Blue Dolphins by Scott O'Dell

The Magician's Nephew by C. S. Lewis

Mrs. Frisby and the Rats of NIMH by Robert C. O'Brien

The Mysterious Benedict Society by Trenton Lee Stewart

On My Honor by Marion Dane Bauer

The Phantom Tollbooth by Norton Juster

The Planet of Junior Brown by Virginia Hamilton

Walk Two Moons by Sharon Creech

A Wizard of Earthsea by Ursula K. Le Guin

Classroom Library Books

All of the read-alouds previously listed are also great for a classroom library. In addition, here are some more books to check out:

Fiction

Adventures on the Ancient Silk Road by Priscilla Galloway with Dawn Hunter

Are You There, God? It's Me, Margaret by Judy Blume

Calvin and Hobbes (series) by Bill Watterson

Captain Underpants (series) by Dav Pilkey

The Chronicles of Narnia (series) by C. S. Lewis

Code Talker: A Novel About the Navajo Marines of World War Two by Joseph Bruchac

The Dreamer by Pam Muñoz Ryan

Eragon by Christopher Paolini

Harry Potter (series) by J. K. Rowling

The Hobbit by J. R. R. Tolkien

Holes by Louis Sachar

Journey to Topaz: A Story of the Japanese-American Evacuation by Yoshiko Uchida

The Lightning Thief by Rick Riordan

Little House on the Prairie (series) by Laura Ingalls Wilder

Maniac Magee by Jerry Spinelli

Rickshaw Girl by Mitali Perkins

My Side of the Mountain by Jean Craighead George

Seal Child by Sylvia Peck

A Series of Unfortunate Events (series) by Lemony Snicket

The Spiderwick Chronicles (series) by Holly Black and Tony DiTerlizzi

The Tale of Desperaux by Kate DiCamillo

Where the Red Fern Grows by Wilson Rawls

A Wrinkle in Time by Madeleine L'Engle

115

CONTINUED ▶

Classroom Library Books continued

Poetry

Falling Up by Shel Silverstein

Honey, I Love and Other Poems by Eloise Greenfield

Love That Dog by Sharon Creech

One River, Many Creeks: Poems from All Around the World edited by Valerie Bloom

Poems to Dream Together/Poemas Para Soñar Juntos by Francisco X. Alarcón

Poetry for Young People: Maya Angelou edited by Edwin Graves Wilson, PhD (from the *Poetry for Young People* series by Sterling Publishing)

Rainbow World: Poems from Many Cultures edited by Debjani Chatterjee and Bashabi Fraser

Informational Texts and Other Nonfiction

For many fifth graders, reading books of information is their favorite kind of reading. Each year, you'll see students gravitate toward books about animals, outer space, or history, so it's important to have some age-appropriate texts about these and other nonfiction topics.

American Revolution by Stuart Murray (from the *DK Eyewitness Books* series)

As Long as the Rivers Flow by Larry Loyie with Constance Brissenden

The Circuit: Stories from the Life of a Migrant Child by Francisco Jiménez

Graphic Science (series by Capstone Press)

Great Migrations by Elizabeth Carney (National Geographic Kids)

Highlights magazine

A History of US by Joy Hakim (series by Oxford University Press)

If You Lived at the Time of Martin Luther King by Ellen Levine (from the *If You* series by Scholastic)

One World, One Day by Barbara Kerley

Quest for the Tree Kangaroo by Sy Montgomery

Sacagawea: American Pathfinder by Flora Warren Seymour (from the *Childhood of Famous Americans* series by Aladdin Paperbacks)

Sequoyah by James Rumford

We Are the Ship: The Story of Negro League Baseball by Kadir Nelson

Board/Card Games

Backgammon

Bananagrams

Blokus (Mattel)

Brain Quest card decks (Workman)

Chess

Mancala

Monopoly (Hasbro)

Parcheesi

Pictionary (Parker Brothers)

Quiddler (SET Enterprises)

Rummikub (Pressman)

Scattergories (Parker Brothers)

Scrabble (Hasbro)

Set (SET Enterprises)

Websites

Whether you use websites as a choice activity during certain academic periods, something students can use during indoor recess, or as a part of ongoing research projects, it's important to run them by the technology coordinator at school. In fact, many schools need to pre-approve any sites that students are going to use. Here are some of my favorites:

WWW.COOLMATH-GAMES.COM (math fun)

HTTP://STREAMING.DISCOVERYEDUCATION.COM
(resources for teachers, parents, and children)

WWW.EXPLORINGNATURE.ORG (nature and science)

WWW.FUNBRAIN.COM (various activities and games)

WWW.LEARNINGPLANET.COM (resources for teachers and children)

WWW.WORDCENTRAL.COM (dictionary, spelling, and word games)

HTTP://KIDS.NATIONALGEOGRAPHIC.COM
(geography, culture, nature, and lots more)

WWW.SPELLINGCITY.COM (spelling and vocabulary fun)

WWW.TIMEFORKIDS.COM/TFK/KIDS (current events)

ACKNOWLEDGMENTS

As with just about any big project, this book represents a compilation of ideas and efforts from a huge number of people. First and foremost, I'd like to thank the many colleagues who have shaped and influenced my teaching of fifth grade. I've had the honor and privilege of working with incredible fifth grade teachers for much of my career, and I have learned so much from so many different people. The first team of fifth grade teachers I ever saw in action taught me a great deal. From Mike Guarraia, Janie Pressley, and Jane Bates, I learned about humor, rigor, compassion, and dedication. I have also had many fifth grade colleagues since then who have taught me and influenced my thinking and teaching: Jen Dunham, Lori Benincasa, Chris Hall, and many others.

In a more general sense, I would like to thank my parents, Susan Trask and Marion Anderson, and my wife, Heather Anderson, who are all master teachers. They have all been a constant influence on my thinking and teaching, and I continue to enjoy our many talks and discussions about all things education.

The dedicated and inspiring staff at Northeast Foundation for Children have also played a huge role in shaping who I am as a teacher and how this book developed. Margaret Berry Wilson, Alice Yang, Elizabeth Nash, Cathy Hess, Sarah Fillion, and Jim Brissette have all had a huge part to play in the shaping of this book, and Helen Merena's design talents helped bring many of the ideas in this book to life.

Finally, and perhaps most importantly, I would like to thank my family. Heather is an incredible teacher, parent, partner, and friend, and her support and companionship is a constant positive force in my life. My children, Ethan and Carly, keep me grounded in reality and remind me of the strong moral commitment that we all need to have in the shaping of positive school environments—where every child is valued, supported, and challenged.

About the *Responsive Classroom*® Approach

All of the recommended practices in this book come from or are consistent with the *Responsive Classroom* approach. Developed by classroom teachers and backed by independent research, the *Responsive Classroom* approach emphasizes social, emotional, and academic growth in a strong and safe school community. The goal is to enable optimal student learning. Following are strategies within the *Responsive Classroom* approach, along with resources for learning about each.

All these resources are published by Northeast Foundation for Children and available from WWW.RESPONSIVECLASSROOM.ORG ∎ 800-360-6332

Morning Meeting: Gathering as a whole class each morning to greet one another, share news, and warm up for the day ahead

99 Activities and Greetings: Great for Morning Meeting . . . and other meetings, too! by Melissa Correa-Connolly. 2004.

Doing Math in Morning Meeting: 150 Quick Activities That Connect to Your Curriculum by Andy Dousis and Margaret Wilson with an introduction by Roxann Kriete. 2010.

Morning Meeting Activities in a Responsive Classroom DVD. 2008.

The Morning Meeting Book by Roxann Kriete with contributions by Lynn Bechtel. 2002.

Morning Meeting Greetings in a Responsive Classroom DVD. 2008.

Morning Meeting Messages K–6: 180 Sample Charts from Three Classrooms by Rosalea S. Fisher, Eric Henry, and Deborah Porter. 2006.

Sample Morning Meetings in a Responsive Classroom DVD and viewing guide. 2009.

Foundation-Setting During the First Weeks of School: Taking time during the critical first weeks of school to establish expectations, routines, a sense of community, and a positive classroom tone

The First Six Weeks of School by Paula Denton and Roxann Kriete. 2000.

Guided Discovery in a Responsive Classroom DVD. 2010.

Teaching Children to Care: Classroom Management for Ethical and Academic Growth, K–8, revised ed., by Ruth Sidney Charney. 2002.

Positive Teacher Language: Using words and tone as a tool to promote children's active learning, sense of community, and self-discipline

The Power of Our Words: Teacher Language That Helps Children Learn by Paula Denton, EdD. 2007.

Teacher Language in a Responsive Classroom DVD. 2009.

Rule Creation and Logical Consequences: Helping students create classroom rules to ensure an environment that allows all class members to meet their learning goals; responding to rule-breaking in a way that respects students and restores positive behavior

Creating Rules with Students in a Responsive Classroom DVD. 2007.

Rules in School: Teaching Discipline in the Responsive Classroom, 2nd ed., by Kathryn Brady, Mary Beth Forton, and Deborah Porter. 2011.

Interactive Modeling: Teaching children to notice and internalize expected behaviors through a unique modeling technique

Rules in School: Teaching Discipline in the Responsive Classroom, 2nd ed., by Kathryn Brady, Mary Beth Forton, and Deborah Porter. 2011.

Teaching Children to Care: Classroom Management for Ethical and Academic Growth, K–8, revised ed., by Ruth Sidney Charney. 2002.

Classroom Organization: Setting up the physical room in ways that encourage students' independence, cooperation, and productivity

Classroom Spaces That Work by Marlynn K. Clayton with Mary Beth Forton. 2001.

Movement, Games, Songs, and Chants: Sprinkling quick, lively activities throughout the school day to keep students energized, engaged, and alert

16 Songs Kids Love to Sing (book and CD) performed by Pat and Tex LaMountain. 1998.

99 Activities and Greetings: Great for Morning Meeting . . . and other meetings, too! by Melissa Correa-Connolly. 2004.

Doing Math in Morning Meeting: 150 Quick Activities That Connect to Your Curriculum by Andy Dousis and Margaret Wilson with an introduction by Roxann Kriete. 2010.

Energizers! 88 Quick Movement Activities That Refresh and Refocus, K–6 by Susan Lattanzi Roser. 2009.

Morning Meeting Activities in a Responsive Classroom DVD. 2008.

Solving Behavior Problems with Children: Engaging children in solving their behavior problems so they feel safe, challenged, and invested in changing

Solving Thorny Behavior Problems: How Teachers and Students Can Work Together by Caltha Crowe. 2009.

Sammy and His Behavior Problems: Stories and Strategies from a Teacher's Year by Caltha Crowe. 2010. (Also available as an audiobook.)

Working with Families: Hearing parents' insights and helping them understand the school's teaching approaches

Parents & Teachers Working Together by Carol Davis and Alice Yang. 2005.

About Child Development

Understanding children's development is crucial to teaching them well. To learn more about child development, see the following resources:

Child and Adolescent Development for Educators by Michael Pressley and Christine McCormick. Guilford Press. 2007. This textbook presents understandable explanations of theories and research about child development and suggests ways to apply those theories and research to classroom teaching.

Child Development, 8th ed., by Laura E. Berk. Pearson Education, Inc. 2009. This textbook summarizes the history and current thinking about child development in easy-to-understand prose. The author outlines the major theories and research and provides practical guidance for teachers.

Child Development Guide by the Center for Development of Human Services, SUNY, Buffalo State College. 2002. WWW.BSC-CDHS.ORG/ FOSTERPARENTTRAINING/PDFS/CHILDDEVELGUIDE.PDF. The center presents characteristics of children at each stage of development in an easy-to-use guide for foster parents.

"The Child in the Elementary School" by Frederick C. Howe in *Child Study Journal*, Vol. 23: 4. 1993. The author presents the common characteristics of students at each grade level, identified by observing students and gathering teacher observations.

"How the Brain Learns: Growth Cycles of Brain and Mind" by Kurt W. Fischer and Samuel P. Rose in *Educational Leadership*, Vol. 56: 3, pp. 56–60. November 1998. The authors, who blend the study of child development with neuroscience, summarize their prior work in a format intended for educators. They conclude that "both behavior and the brain change in repeating patterns that seem to involve common growth cycles."

"The Scientist in the Crib: A Conversation with Andrew Meltzoff" by Marcia D'Arcangelo in *Educational Leadership*, Vol. 58: 3, pp. 8–13. November 2000. Written in an interview format, this article dispels myths about child development and explores ways in which research about cognitive development might inform the work of educators.

Yardsticks: Children in the Classroom Ages 4–14, 3rd ed., by Chip Wood. Northeast Foundation for Children. 2007. This highly practical book for teachers and parents offers narratives and easy-to-scan charts of children's common physical, social-emotional, cognitive, and language characteristics at each age from four through fourteen and notes the classroom implications of these characteristics.

Your Child: Emotional, Behavioral, and Cognitive Development from Birth through Preadolescence by AACAP (American Academy of Child and Adolescent Psychiatry) and David Pruitt, MD. Harper Paperbacks. 2000. Intended for parents, this book presents information about children's development and the characteristics of each stage and offers tips for helping children develop appropriately.

122

ABOUT THE AUTHOR

 **Mike Anderson** is a *Responsive Classroom*® consultant with Northeast Foundation for Children and has been presenting *Responsive Classroom* workshops since 1999. Mike taught third, fourth, and fifth grades for fifteen years in Connecticut and New Hampshire. In 2004, he was the recipient of a Milken National Educator Award for excellence in teaching.

Mike is the author of two other books in the *What Every Teacher Needs to Know* series (third grade and fourth grade), plus *The Well-Balanced Teacher* (ASCD, 2010) and *The Research-Ready Classroom* (with co-author Andy Dousis; Heinemann, 2006). Mike lives in Durham, New Hampshire, with his wife, Heather, and their two children, Ethan and Carly.

ABOUT THE PUBLISHER

Northeast Foundation for Children, Inc., a not-for-profit educational organization, is the developer of the *Responsive Classroom*® approach to teaching. We offer the following for elementary school educators:

PUBLICATIONS AND RESOURCES

■ Books, CDs, and DVDs for teachers and school leaders

■ Professional development kits for school-based study

■ Website with extensive library of free articles: WWW.RESPONSIVECLASSROOM.ORG

■ Free quarterly newsletter for elementary educators

■ The *Responsive*™ blog, with news, ideas, and advice from and for elementary educators

PROFESSIONAL DEVELOPMENT SERVICES

■ Introductory one-day workshops for teachers and administrators

■ Week-long institutes offered nationwide each summer and on-site at schools

■ Follow-up workshops and on-site consulting services to support implementation

■ Development of teacher leaders to support schoolwide implementation

■ Resources for site-based study

■ National conference for administrators and teacher leaders

FOR DETAILS, CONTACT:

Responsive Classroom®

Northeast Foundation for Children, Inc.
85 Avenue A, Suite 204, P.O. Box 718
Turners Falls, Massachusetts 01376-0718

800-360-6332 ■ www.responsiveclassroom.org
info@responsiveclassroom.org